BLESSINGS AND BETRAYALS

A TRUE STORY OF ONE WOMAN'S FIGHT FOR FREEDOM AND LOVE

Good Luck

BLESSINGS AND BETRAYALS

A TRUE STORY OF ONE WOMAN'S FIGHT FOR FREEDOM AND LOVE

BY

R J BLUM

www.bookstandpublishing.com

Published by
Bookstand Publishing
Morgan Hill, CA 95037
4592_7

Cover Photo: R J Blum
Editors: Gloria Beverage and Sue Clark

ISBN 978-1-63498-634-2

Library of Congress Control Number: 2018930620

Printed in the United States of America

Author's Note

What follows is the story of our family, based on the experiences I lived, things described to me, activities I have observed, my feelings and the feelings reported to me by others. I have recalled events and conversations to the best of my ability. I now know what happened to our family does not have to be repeated. This story contains my opinions, and my hope that awareness gained from Blessings and Betrayals, will prevent others from losing their freedom and love. I have changed names to protect identities.

A Joy Forever New

Please don't sing sad songs for me,

Forget your grief and fears,

For I am in a perfect place,

Away from pain and tears.

I'm far away from hunger

And hurt and want and pride,

I have a place in Heaven

With the Master at my side

My life on earth was very good,

As earthly lives can go,

But Paradise is so much more

Than anyone can know.

My heart is filled with happiness

And sweet rejoicing, too.

To walk with God is perfect peace,

A joy forever new.

—Unknown

Dedicated In Loving Memory Of Helen Patterson

Acknowledgements

I want to thank my friends Betes Flores and Julian Hubbard for their encouragement and help. You believed I could write Blessings and Betrayals before I did.

I also want to thank my early readers Jackie Pokorny, and my daughter. Your suggestions were invaluable.

Thank you to my editors Gloria Beverage and Sue Clark. You taught me so much.

A special thank you to my husband, Mike Blum, who gave me the time and space I needed to write a book.

Contents

There is no crueler tyranny than that which is perpetuated under the shield of law and in the name of justice.
—Charles de Montesquieu

One loyal friend is worth ten thousand relatives.
—Euripides

Families are the compass that guides us. They are the inspiration to reach great heights, and our comfort when we occasionally falter.
—Brad Henry

Health is not valued till sickness comes.
—Dr. Thomas Fuller

Unprepared

There is no crueler tyranny than that which is perpetuated under the shield of law and in the name of justice.
—Charles de Montesquieu

I approached the double doors of the probate courtroom, I was nervous. My hand shook a little as I opened the door and held it for Grandma Elena to walk through. Maneuvering a walker made her stoop over, but it did not take away any of her pride and determination. A couple of friends, who had come in support, followed us inside. We sat in the back of the courtroom on the right. Grandma Elena's court-appointed attorney was talking in the hall with her son, Ralph, and his attorney. Ralph's wife Doris, and youngest daughter Cynthia, were already seated close to the front of the courtroom.

Doris and Cynthia turned around in their seats long enough to stare at Grandma Elena as we entered. If looks could kill, there would have been a lot of dead bodies in the courtroom that day. When Grandma Elena sat down, she was drilling holes in the back of their heads with her clear blue eyes.

Soon everyone was seated.

Other conservatorship cases were called. No one was fighting those actions. The judge granted the requests without discussion.

Grandma Elena's well-respected court-appointed attorney had an impressive multi-page resume. After the first hearing, he told Grandma Elena if she didn't like the way he was handling the case she could replace him. She had already tried.

Her case was called.

Grandma Elena insisted on walking from the gallery to the defense table. She stood next to her attorney, even though he told her she could remain seated. I watched her walk forward, defiant, as close to a power walk as anyone can have while using a walker. Her attorney was bent over looking at his papers on the table as she stood beside him. After the first hearing he'd stated that he believed all old people needed to be conserved, so he did not fight to block the conservatorship. At the prosecution table stood Ralph and his attorney, Enrique Rodriguez. They looked straight ahead at Judge Conway.

When the judge began, Grandma Elena interrupted him. "Can I speak, Judge?"

I held my breath.

"Yes, take your time."

I was nervous for Grandma Elena, but proud to watch her stand and fight. Grandma Elena told me when we entered the courtroom that she was afraid, although I couldn't see her fear. She outlined what she wanted with a clear and coherent statement.

Grandma Elena was, opposed to being placed under conservatorship. And yet if that happened, she didn't want Ralph to be her conservator. "There are too many negative feelings between us," Grandma Elena had said.

She was fighting to continue to live in her home of fifty years, surrounded by love from friends, neighbors, and my family. She wanted to sit in her favorite chair, read, watch the birds and squirrels in the back garden, and listen to the rain drops hit the patio cover.

Grandma Elena told the judge sometimes she had trouble remembering things. She had completed nine hours of testing with a psychologist, and asked him to review the report. Grandma Elena told him, "I've done many things and I've lived many places in ninety years. May I ask my son a question?"

"Yes, go ahead."

"Why are you doing this to me?"

Ralph continued to look straight ahead and didn't answer.

I could not speak. I was not a family member by blood or marriage, but one adopted out of love. Our forty years of friendship had no standing with the court. The fact that she had been Grandmother to my children was not considered.

Judge Conway, poker faced and with gavel in hand, said, "I will continue the temporary conservatorship for thirty days while you obtain a second physiological evaluation."

We gathered our things to leave, and I wondered, how and when a fractured family relationship became a legal war?

Growing a Friendship

One loyal friend is worth ten thousand relatives.
—Euripides

On a bright spring day in 1974, my college friend Monica, my 6-month-old daughter Charlotte, and I were having a garage sale and we struck up conversations with passersby.

When Grandma Elena walked by with her two beagles, Roxy and Dolly, she stopped to talk with us. Charlotte was in her playpen, the things we had for sale were on tables on both sides of her.

Grandma Elena looked over at me and asked with a smile, "How much for the baby?"

"It depends on the day." I chuckled. "Today she's golden." Just then Charlotte reached for Grandma Elena and smiled.

Intrigued with Charlotte, Grandma Elena said she would take her dogs home and be back to play with the baby. When she returned, she picked up Charlotte, talking and cooing at her. She tickled Charlotte's feet by bouncing them on the grass. I was happy to have her fuss over my baby. Before she left that day, Grandma Elena made sure I knew which house was hers and stressed she was available to babysit. She explained she worked for a major corporation hiring hourly employees, but her evenings and weekends were open.

She seemed nice and only lived four houses down the street, so the next week, while my husband Adam was attending an evening class, Charlotte and I went to visit Grandma Elena and her family. When Grandma Elena answered the door, her face broke into a broad smile and her eyes lit up. I walked into her house. Books were stacked on every flat surface. The bookcases on the wall were overflowing. The books weren't popular novels, but classics, references, histories, biographies. It felt familiar because, my grandma's house was filled with the same kinds of books.

Why would a 26-year-old woman develop a forty-year friendship with a woman of 52? Grandma Elena shared my passion for children.

When I was small and adults would ask, "What do you want to be when you grow up?" I always answered, "A mommy." At 20 I married Adam, who shared my passion for a family. I finished my bachelor degree and got a job with a start-up called Intel. We bought a house, made improvements, and began to buy furniture. We were making our nest. Everything we did was to prepare for me to be a stay at home mom. Charlotte's birth was the culmination of my life-long dream. She was my own little miracle.

Grandma Elena had followed her Navy husband all over the world, keeping her family together. When the boys were half grown she practiced her shorthand and typing so she could take a job with a major corporation as an executive secretary. Her goal was to create savings so her sons could attend college.

She shared that her two sons, Gene, 30, and Ralph, 27, were unmarried. This meant it would be some time before they would present her with grandchildren. To fill the void, she had set a goal of finding grandchildren to adopt.

I was the daughter Grandma Elena and Papa Frank never had. Grandma Elena was my friend, my confidant, my mentor, as well as a loving grandmother to my children and a surrogate mother to me. She supported my choice to be a mommy. My mother was career oriented and very critical of my choice.

Grandma Elena began inviting Charlotte to play at her house. She had found her grandchild. From then on Grandma Elena attended birthday parties, religious celebrations, performances, games, and school functions — every marker in our lives. Together, Grandma Elena and Papa Frank stepped into the role of grandparents, celebrating our family's triumphs and commiserating with us in our defeats.

By November, Grandma Elena, Papa Frank, and Ralph joined us for Charlotte's first birthday celebration. Uncle Ralph built Charlotte a beautiful indoor wooden slide the ideal size for a toddler, a true labor of love. It would be used by all three of my children. Grandma Elena gave Charlotte a special gift, a board book with pictures of baby animals. Not just any board book of baby animals, but an exact copy of the book Charlotte and Grandma Elena shared during their visits. Charlotte loved the book so much she wouldn't put it down. When I tried to take it so she could open the rest of her presents, she burst into tears.

As I prepared to welcome our second child, I began to make things our second baby would need. Grandma Elena never let me forget the afternoon I called for help with a crochet problem. I knew the basics of crochet. I had used it to edge knitting projects a few times. However, on that day, I had gone to the local yarn store and found a pattern for a crocheted christening gown and blanket. I bought the supplies for both items, and had tried to start the gown. Even though I didn't know if I was having a boy or girl, I thought the gown was neutral. I had crocheted my chain and then patterned the first row. The next instruction said turn. Turn how? I had never encountered this instruction. Edgings start at one end and stop at the other. There is no turn. That's when I called Grandma Elena. "I need you to look at this crochet problem." Since Grandma Elena was experienced with crocheting, I knew she could help me. She told me to bring it to her house.

When I arrived she said, "What's the problem?"

"Turn, how do you do it?"

She grabbed the end and flipped it over, "Like that."

"That's the back."

"There is no back in crochet."

"There is in knitting."

"You're not knitting. What are you making?"

I showed her the pattern and the yarn for the project.

"What have you crocheted before?"

I confessed, "Just edges."

"Most people start with a doily or a pot holder...something small. Do you think you can finish this?"

"I better. I spent two hundred dollars on this yarn."

"If you finish this, I'll believe you can do anything," she said with a hearty laugh.

I did finish and put it away to wait for our baby's arrival.

After that, every time I talked about crocheting, Grandma Elena reminded me of my "jump into the ocean without knowing how to swim" approach.

When Grandma Elena went in for surgery in early April 1975, I assured her I would do whatever I could to help. A couple of hours after Papa Frank brought her home, I checked on her, bringing her flowers along with Charlotte. Papa Frank took Charlotte in his arms as we walked through the front door. I made my way to the bedroom where Grandma Elena was resting. She was doing well, but appreciated having another woman help her to the bathroom and back to bed. I took the phone from the head of the bed and put it next to her in case she needed to call me. I returned every couple of hours the first days to be sure Grandma Elena was comfortable.

An early morning phone call alerted me to an emergency at Grandma Elena's house where I found her sitting on the couch in tears. Her breasts were swollen with hot spots — all the symptoms of a breast infection. She was in a great deal of pain. At nine o'clock, we got through to the doctor's office and they agreed to see her right away.

Grandma Elena could not get dressed. Clothing touching her body was excruciating so I suggested she wear her lightweight robe.

I learned that women with Grandma Elena's medical history should not take certain hormone replacement drugs. Prescribing that medication resulted in a painful and avoidable condition. While the doctor had gone over her medical history before surgery and noted it on her chart, he had been in a hurry afterwards, and did not recheck the chart. That morning he changed her medication, but failed to acknowledge the mistake or apologize. The medication did not threaten her life, but it did create a great deal of unnecessary pain and suffering. After that scare, Grandma Elena decided to change doctors.

In mid-April, I had my own medical emergency. Climbing into bed late one Saturday night I felt wet. I thought my water had broken, and yet, my baby was not due until the end of June. Lights were on at my neighbors, so I knocked and asked if I could move sleeping Charlotte into the crib I knew Nancy and her sister Jeanie kept for their godchild. Adam took me to the hospital, but the attending nurse told me I had just lost bladder control. Embarrassed, I left without waiting for the doctor. Once at home, I collected Charlotte and we all went to bed.

The next morning when we got up, I realized I had left my purse at the hospital. A quick call confirmed they had it at the nurse's station. Adam offered to get it and suggested he would take us out for a nice breakfast. Grandma Elena was watering her flowers and saw the early morning activity. She called to check on us. I told her what had happened and asked how she felt. She indicated her doctor did not want her to resume normal activities, including lifting.

Jeanie, our next-door neighbor, came to invite Charlotte to play with her goddaughter.

While standing talking to Jeanie, my legs became covered in blood. That time I knew it was not a loss of bladder control. Jeanie took Charlotte while I went inside to call the doctor. I had one gush, with no pain or labor, so the doctor told me to stay quiet and see if it happened again.

I sat at the dining room table for about an hour. Then it happened. Everything broke loose. On my way to the phone, I stuck my head out the door to the garage and called to Adam, who was rotating the car tires.

"How fast can you have the car back together?"

"Give me two minutes. Why?" He had decided to keep himself busy to control his nervousness about events inside the house.

"I think we need the car."

After the call to the doctor, I called my mother. I told her what had happened and asked her to come and stay with Charlotte. I was not surprised when she said she would have to check her work schedule for availability. I hoped she would help me. Even in an emergency, she wasn't into the grandmother thing. No surprise since she had never been into the mother thing, either.

Next, I called Daddy. By then, my shaky resolve was failing me. The minute I heard his voice I started to sob. Daddy traveled the world for work, but this time, we were on the same continent.

"Daddy, I'm in trouble here. There's something wrong. I think it's the baby."

"What happened? Do you need me to come? Where is your mother?"

"She's home. She's checking her work schedule to see if she has some time. I need her to watch Charlotte while I'm at the hospital. I'm not sure what is going on, but I'm sure it's not good."

"Honey, don't worry, your mother will be there. Just take care of yourself."

"Thank you, Daddy, that's all I need. I'll make sure someone calls you as soon as we know anything."

I hated going behind my mother's back, but I needed help and I knew Daddy would convince her when I couldn't.

The story of my life — the parent willing to help didn't have the skills and the parent with the skills was reluctant to step in.

I tried to clean myself up, but it didn't go well. The shower resembled the scene from Psycho. Out of the shower, I stood straddling a plastic pan to catch the dripping blood and tried not to give in to the terror I felt. As I tried to get dressed, I began to feel weak and sat on the edge of the bed. My neighbor Jeanie brought Charlotte into the bedroom to say good-bye. I gave her a hug and said I would be back as soon as I could. Jeanie tried to comfort me as I sat crying, assuring me she would keep Charlotte until my mother arrived the next morning.

By the time I got to the front door, I was soaked in blood. At the hospital, the nurse helped me into a gown. Adam was asked to wait in the hall. When my doctor examined me, he was amazed labor had not begun. He told us he did not see how our baby would survive.

After he left the room I burst into tears.

"Why are you crying?"

"You heard. Our baby is going to die."

"Not dead, yet," Adam announced with surety.

I held tight to those words. Five days later, many tests and a move to a hospital with a bed in the neonatal unit, Ethan arrived. Huge for being born two months early, Ethan weighed in at four pounds, eight ounces. He would thrive but remained in the hospital for 21 days.

After three days, I was sent home with instructions not to lift, which made it impossible to care for Charlotte by myself. My mother left two days after I got home, in spite of my restrictions. Grandma Elena, who was still recovering from her surgery, stepped up and filled the void left by my mother. She claimed her doctor had released her from all restrictions. I remained skeptical, yet thankful.

Grandma Elena came by every morning and helped me get 17-month-old Charlotte dressed and fed. Then the two would go for a walk. Some days the pair took several walks.

The day before Ethan's release from the hospital, Grandma Elena stopped by and asked Charlotte if she wanted to take another walk. Charlotte loved those walks. Then Grandma Elena came into the bedroom with Charlotte right behind her. I started updating Grandma Elena on Ethan's condition. Charlotte, tired of waiting, began patting Grandma Elena on the knee saying, "walk, walk."

Grandma Elena said, "Yes, sweetheart, in just a minute."

Our conversation went on too long. All of a sudden, Charlotte insisted, "Gama, I want to take a walk."

Grandma Elena stopped mid-sentence and replied, "If you're going to say it in a full sentence, we'll go right now."

Charlotte's first sentence and she said it to Grandma Elena.

"Frustrate the child enough and she will speak in full sentences." I laughed.

Grandma Elena's son, Ralph, married Doris the week Ethan was born. That summer as Ralph, Doris, and I walked up the street between my house and Grandma Elena's, they expressed their gratitude, that Grandma Elena's attachment to my children had taken the pressure off them to start their family.

Two years later, Doris volunteered to babysit Ethan two mornings a month in the fall while I worked at the Parent Pre-School Charlotte attended. Since Ralph and Doris did not have children yet, there was no opportunity to reciprocate. I tried to warn Doris that Ethan was suffering from separation anxiety. He cried from the moment he realized I was leaving until I returned. He continued the behavior the entire semester.

Doris tried watching Sesame Street with him. She placed his toys and a snack within his reach. She tried to read stories to him, but he was very stubborn. Each time I returned, I questioned whether Doris wanted to watch him again. Ethan's behavior remained unchanged. I will always be grateful to Doris for her selfless help.

The next semester, my friend and fellow carpool mom was back from maternity leave. We decided to trade babysitting, which solved the problem of child care for both of us. While Ethan continued to have separation anxiety, the lure of seeing a new baby seemed to console him.

Although the walking tradition continued with all three children, the first walks stand out in my memory. One night, just before Charlotte turned two, the wind blew all the autumn leaves off the trees and covered the lawns and sidewalk. Grandma Elena and Charlotte bundled up for their walk, but as they stepped out the front door, Charlotte stopped in her tracks.

"Grandma Elena, we need to get the glue and you can put me on your shoulders so I can reach and glue the leaves back on the trees."

After that, I don't think an autumn passed that Grandma Elena didn't ask Charlotte if she was ready to glue the leaves back on the trees.

On their walks around the neighborhood, Charlotte and Grandma Elena had designated landmarks. They passed one of the neighbor's landscaping projects that took a long time to finish. Charlotte called it "Big Mess." She could not pass one of the neighbor's yards that had a rock landscape feature, without touching her "Pet Rock."

They also checked to see if "Gucky was home." The dog liked to stick his nose under the fence in his front yard, when they walked by, which amused my toddler.

The spring Charlotte was 3½, she and Grandma Elena headed for the swings at our school park. As they entered the back gate, and started to walk across the field to the swings, Grandma Elena felt Charlotte tugging on her hand. She looked down to see the distressed look on Charlotte's face.

"What's wrong?"

Charlotte replied, "Grandma Elena, doggy poop everywhere."

The night before, the maintenance crew had aerated the lawn, to allow the grass to breath. They had left the plugs of dirt exposed on the grass.

As the years went by, we banked great memories. Grandma Elena and I found we had many common interests beyond my children. The truth is, we enjoyed each other's company.

There was a bond with Papa Frank. I always thought of Papa Frank as a teddy bear. He was gentle, quiet, big, and strong with powerful hands. He told me he got a job washing dishes after he graduated from high school. One night, walking home from work, he saw a recruitment poster that said, "Uncle Sam Wants You," and at that moment he knew he wanted to join the Navy.

I think he enjoyed working with his hands. He made and repaired many things. He welded re-bar to fashion frames and legs for living room tables and fitted each one with a glass top. He was an excellent mechanic. He could repair any vehicle. He also made things out of wood — toys, gates, fences, patio covers.

Papa Frank replaced all the plumbing pipes in their house with upgraded copper pipes. His next project was to re-roof the house. The local lumber yard delivered shingles, roofing paper, and other supplies. The local refuse company delivered a bin to collect the old roofing materials.

He started early in the morning tearing off a section at a time. Papa Frank threw the old shingles and roofing paper to the ground. Grandma Elena and I gathered up the refuse and deposited it in the bin on the driveway. I was happy to work with them. After Grandma Elena and I finished, we went inside for a cup of coffee and a chat.

Grandma Elena called one day to say Papa Frank needed help. She explained he wanted to destroy a wasp nest in the bushes on the side of the house and he wanted me to stand by with the hose. If the wasps began to swarm him, he would call for me to hose him down. She refused when he asked her to help, and suggested I would be wise to do the same thing. While I countered that professionals are equipped for that kind of work, I agreed to help him. What could go wrong?

When I got to their house, I found Grandma Elena and Papa Frank in the garage. He was wearing two pairs of coveralls, boots, gloves, and a beekeeper's hat. Grandma Elena had helped him duct tape his gloves, boots, and hat to the outside of his coveralls. He looked like he was ready to walk on the moon.

Grandma Elena went inside as Papa Frank and I walked around to the side of the house. He handed me the hose. I watched as he began to tackle the bush with the wasp nest. After a couple of minutes, he yelled at me to hose him down. I turned the water on him. It only took seconds for the wasps to gather above the water spray. Then they turned and headed straight for me. I was wearing no protection — only a t-shirt, shorts, and sandals. I panicked, yelled, "Every man for himself," dropped the hose, ran around the end of the house and through the garage. I burst through the kitchen door, slamming it behind me and slumped into a chair.

I was breathless as I exclaimed, "Grandma Elena, it was so scary. It was like being in a horror movie, probably one called 'The Swarm of the Killer Wasps.'"

When Grandma Elena asked what had happened, I explained the wasps had started swarming toward me.

"I told you to be careful," she said.

"You did."

"I told you his ideas don't always work like he expects."

"You did and next time I will listen more carefully."

Just then, Papa Frank came in the kitchen.

"Are they swarming in the garage?" I said.

"No. I got rid of the nest. Will you girls help me out of this extra coverall? It's getting hot."

We were amazed how many layers of clothing the wasps had been able to crawl under before they died. We found them inside his gloves and socks. In fact, a couple of them were still alive. Papa Frank left to take a shower and change his clothes.

Grandma Elena offered me a cup of tea, saying I looked like I needed one. I truly did. After finishing the tea, I ventured outside, watching for wasps. A few were still flying around where the nest had been. They hadn't gotten the memo.

While I learned to knit as a young girl, Grandma Elena had learned to crochet as a child and knit as an adult. She telephoned one afternoon.

"Jo Ann, do you have a few minutes? I have a knitting problem." When I got to her house and examined her work, it looked like the problem started about four rows back. The only way to fix the problem and keep the correct tension was to take out the four rows.

"Okay, can you do that?"

"Sure." I pulled the needles out of the stitches and began to unravel the offending rows. I looked up to see horror on Grandma Elena's face. "No worries," I said. "It will be back on the needles in a minute."

As I handed the corrected project back to her, the look of relief on Grandma Elena's face was wonderful.

Each September the city hosted a Wine and Art Festival, held within walking distance of our homes. Grandma Elena and I loved to attend. However, we realized the walk back with our purchases presented a challenge.

Grandma Elena came up with the perfect solution. Early on the morning of the festival, she'd drive close to the area, park her car, and then walk home. When the fair opened we'd walk there, spend, several hours, fill her car with our purchases and drive home. We loved seeing the crafts other people produced, and we enjoyed buying items we didn't have the skills or tools to make. We also had fun gathering ideas from the many creative vendors.

We didn't share interests in every craft. Grandma Elena liked to make fancy paper decorations called Scherenschnitte. I didn't think I wanted to put so much time into cutting intricate paper designs. The worst problem centered on the special scissors made for right-handed individuals. I am left handed and cannot cut simple designs with right handed scissors. Grandma Elena and Charlotte did share a love for the paper designs. I still have the framed design Charlotte gave me on Mother's Day when she was twelve.

Grandma Elena often wondered if she had had a daughter, would she have developed different interests. She talked about how she didn't like shopping, so would ask me to go with her. I was with her when she picked out the new carpet for her house, the end tables, coffee table for the living room, the living room drapes, and the Stiffel lamp.

Over the years, I'd shop for Grandma Elena while I was doing my own errands. Grandma Elena would reimburse me.

My mother criticized my choice to be a stay-at-home mom. She was adamant. The responsibilities of being a mother had interfered with her own career goals. Grandma Elena, on the other hand, was very supportive of my choice. Her support brought us closer together.

More than Friends — Family

Families are the compass that guides us.
They are the inspiration to reach great heights,
and our comfort when we occasionally falter.
—Brad Henry

Grandma Elena and I depended on each other during medical emergencies. Ethan's difficult birth had not erased my desire for a third child. When I mentioned it to Grandma Elena, she expressed the same concern that Adam and my doctor had. Grandma Elena said she and Papa Frank had wanted more children after Ralph was born, but were told there were medical reasons that made it unwise. Grandma Elena did not agree with my decision to try for a third child and she had well founded fears. I was respectful but disagreed. I'd hoped she would agree with me.

When Grandma Elena got the call saying Papa Frank had been taken to the hospital, she called me to go with her. At the hospital, we found Papa Frank in excruciating pain, waiting to be taken to surgery to have his gall bladder removed. Grandma Elena was afraid he was having a heart attack.

She asked, "Where's the pain?"

He indicated an area on his side.

She then reached out to touch him close to the center of his chest, asking, "Is it here?"

He jumped in extreme pain and said, "No."

She then asked, "Are you sure?" and reached for him again.

She stopped before she could touch him when I said, "I think it is better to leave him alone."

She looked at me and then began to reach for him again. At that moment, Papa Frank grabbed her wrist and said, "Mama, sit down, shut up, and enjoy your visit."

While he was in surgery we went to the café and I reassured her that everything would soon be back to normal.

Papa Frank's first heart attack, in 1978 during a spring fishing trip near Lake Siskiyou, came as a shock. Gene and Ralph took Grandma Elena to Lake Siskiyou Hospital. The boys brought the fishing gear back, while Grandma Elena waited with Papa Frank. Once he was cleared, Ralph returned to pick up his parents.

I filled their house with fresh food and flowers. I picked up the books that had been stacked on the bedroom floor and stored them in the bathtub in the front bathroom. Grandma Elena and Papa Frank used the shower in the master bath. Grandma Elena said no one used the front bathtub. We had a good laugh about my choice for book storage. It remained a long-standing joke between us.

Early in the morning of February 15, 1979, I received a call from the American Consulate in Germany saying Daddy had collapsed while waiting for the bus to the airport. They thought he had died and wanted me to come and claim his remains. When I asked where he was, they told me the name of the hospital. I called and found out he was still alive. I was desperate to get there, but didn't have a passport. On my way to the airport, I stopped at the federal building to beg for an emergency passport. I was issued a passport even though I didn't have the proper documents. I believe they checked my story with the American Consulate. I'd never be caught without a valid passport again.

Megan, three months old and still nursing, was about to make her first international trip. The harrowing flight in bad weather over the Atlantic Ocean, with a delay in London, almost left us stranded for an extra day. Twenty-five days after I arrived in Germany, Daddy's condition had improved. The doctors declared him stable and strong enough to return to the U.S. Daddy spent a week in the hospital back in the states while I turned the nursery into a room for him.

Daddy lived with us for several months until he felt strong enough to live on his own, but he never returned to Germany. I wanted him to stay with us. I respected his desire for independent living, and helped him find furniture to make his one-bedroom apartment comfortable.

In an attempt to return to a normal life, I incorporated traditional activities in our daily lives. One activity was getting Megan's picture taken. Grandma Elena and I took Megan to the local photographer. During our stay in Germany, Megan had become accustomed to being held when she was awake. Now she cried whenever I set her down. At the photographer's studio, I sat her on the table, but she just held out her hands, squared off her lower lip and started to cry. Grandma Elena said, "Take the picture."

The photographer responded she was not allowed to take pictures of crying babies. "No one buys them."

Grandma Elena told the photographer she would buy it and did. That photo hung in Grandma Elena's office for years.

The next spring, Papa Frank had his second heart attack, again while fishing. By now I felt like I had lots of experience rescuing heart attack victims. This time, Grandma Elena and I drove together to pick Papa Frank up. We had to wait a couple of days until he was able to make the car ride home. I drove while Grandma Elena gripped her purse on her lap turning her knuckles white. Papa Frank moved around in the back seat in an effort to get comfortable.

Everyone was sad to see the end of Papa Frank's fishing days.

Three years after my frantic trip to Germany, March 1982, I found Daddy had died sleeping in his chair. With 3-year-old Megan in tow, I had gone to his apartment to check on him. I could see him through the sliding glass door and asked a passerby to call 911. I knew I was too late. I had known since Germany that it wouldn't be long. Still, it was a shock to find him. Time allows the pain to change, but the loss is still as great. Daddy had always been there for me and now he was gone. Although I knew I had to go on without him, I was not sure how I would function.

For now, I had to take care of practical things. I called Papa Frank to come get Megan. Grandma Elena was at work, where she hired all the hourly employees for a large local corporation. Papa Frank kept Megan at their house until I collected her at dinner time.

While putting Megan in her evening bath, I noticed a new bruise.

"How did this happen?"

She replied, "When Papa Frank stopped too fast, I fell where your feet go in the truck."

"Weren't you wearing your seat belt?"

"No, Papa Frank put it on me after he picked me up and put me back on the seat. He said not to tell you or Grandma Elena."

"Yes, we won't tell Grandma Elena. She would be very upset with him."

In the days following Daddy's death, Grandma Elena and Papa Frank were magnanimous. Papa Frank arranged for the Masonic Lodge to provide the service, and Grandma Elena found a bagpipe player. We were able to bury Daddy at the mountain's summit in Skylawn Memorial Park, Half Moon Bay. As we walked in for the service, Ethan, almost seven, said to me, "I want to carry the box."

"What box?" I had no idea what he was talking about.

"The box they put Papa in."

"I don't think they'll let a little kid be a pallbearer," I told him.

I had him take a seat and went to talk to the funeral director who replied, "The middle man on each side doesn't have to lift so Ethan can be a pallbearer." I asked Ethan why he wanted to carry the coffin.

His reply was simple. "It's the last thing I can do for Papa."

"You can do it if you still want."

He looked at me, grabbed the lapels of his suit jacket and said, "That's why I'm wearing these stupid clothes."

For days after the service, I wandered around in a fog, doing routine things and trying not to think. I found it so hard to believe Daddy was gone.

Life did go on. Grandma Elena and Papa Frank had become an integral part of our family. When Charlotte wanted to camp out with her friend in front of the apartment building at the end of our street, I said no. She went to the higher court of Grandma Elena, who said, "Children love to camp out."

I explained the girls could camp in our fully fenced backyard. "I don't think two little girls are safe sleeping in a tent on a lawn anyone can walk across."

"Oh, you're right. I couldn't agree more. They can camp in our fenced backyard if they want." Grandma Elena often gave me the perspective of another point of view. After all, she had raised two boys. This time she agreed with me.

Charlotte wasn't giving up. She went to the court of last resort, her dad. When Adam asked me why I objected to something she had her heart set on, I explained, "Grandma Elena and I agree it's not safe. They can camp in one of our backyards."

He was shocked. Grandma Elena hadn't sided with Charlotte. "I'll tell Charlotte tomorrow she can't do it."

When Megan was old enough to play soccer, not just watch her siblings from the sidelines, she asked with pride if Grandma Elena could attend her next game.

Grandma Elena arrived for the early Saturday morning game with coffee in hand. At the first break, the coach came over and asked me, "Who's the kid you brought today? She looks like Megan, but she plays so much more aggressively. What's different?"

I pointed to Grandma Elena. "Grandma came today."

He looked at Grandma Elena and asked, "Can you come to every game?"

Too Sick to be Scared

Health is not valued till sickness comes.
—Dr. Thomas Fuller

The day after Thanksgiving in 1988, I finished the laundry and prepared to put up Christmas decorations. By noon, I sat down to rest. An hour later, I crawled into bed. Adam was amazed to find me so sick when he got home. I had been fine when he left for the office. On Saturday, our doctor had office hours in the morning, so Adam made an appointment and drove me to see him. The doctor determined I had a raging case of pneumonia and started me on antibiotics.

In the middle of the night, my fever spiked to 105°F. Adam woke me as he stumbled around the bedroom.

"Adam, what are you doing?"

"I'm looking for my car keys. I awoke with this pain in my chest and I can't get it to go away. I thought I might drive myself over to the emergency room. The doctors there can examine me and tell my doctor what's wrong so he can give me something."

At that point, the fever had interfered with my ability to think straight. "How did you try to get the pain to go away? What did you do?"

Adam explained, "First I jogged around the block and when it didn't work, I did pushups in the living room."

My foggy response was, "Okay, take the spare keys on the hook and go. No, wait. Are you light headed?"

"No."

"Are you dizzy?"

"No."

"Then go."

I went back to sleep. A couple of hours later, I woke up and noticed he had not come home. Busy night at the ER, I thought, and went back to sleep.

Just before seven, the phone rang. When I answered, the ER doctor began speaking. Convinced I knew what he was going to say, I was only half listening. I began thinking Adam had come in complaining of chest pains and they had run tests. He had indigestion, but was otherwise fine. I snapped to attention when my thoughts and the doctor's words did not match. Unable to untangle what the doctor was saying, I asked, "Are you going to admit him?"

He took a deep breath and said in a most exasperated voice, "My dear, not only am I admitting him, I am going to do the procedures I have just described."

"Right." I was beginning to absorb the information. Adam was having a massive heart attack and the doctors had scheduled an angiogram to discover where the clot in his artery was. Depending on where they located the clot and how much obstruction of blood flow they found, the doctors planned to perform an angioplasty or bypass surgery.

The doctor then said, "My dear, I understand you are ill. Please stay where you are."

"Okay." To tell the truth, I was too sick to go anywhere. I hung up and just stared at the phone.

The full impact of what had happened to Adam was sinking in. Adam had had a massive heart attack at age 43. At this point in a crisis, in the past, I would have called Daddy for support, but Daddy had been gone for six years. I was so grateful that Grandma Elena and Papa Frank were part of our lives. They had stepped into the void Daddy left. Grandma Elena was there to support me in a crisis and I was beginning to realize a big crisis was hitting us full force. I looked at the clock to see if I could call without waking anyone. I picked up the phone and called Grandma Elena.

Grandma Elena had trouble comprehending what I was saying and made me repeat it. It didn't make sense that a man 43 would have a heart attack and drive himself to the hospital. But that's what happened. I'm pretty sure the jogging and pushups had not helped his condition. Grandma Elena arrived within minutes. She took care of everything — the children, the household chores, me, including getting my new prescription. I was becoming weaker.

Ralph took Charlotte, Ethan, and Megan to see their father before he went into surgery. Multiple doctors called to tell me they did not want me at the hospital. They assured me triple bypass surgery was no more dangerous than removing tonsils. I nodded off and a short time later, the phone rang again and the doctors insisted I come to the hospital. Grandma Elena drove me. As I got off the elevator, the nurse at the station facing the elevators looked up. "You must be the sick wife. I'll get you a wheelchair."

Adam's room was just a few steps from the elevator. I sat next to the bed. Adam and I exchanged simple pleasantries trying to reassure each other that everything was going to be fine. He then handed me a stack of papers and said, "The doctors want me to sign these. I told them you handle all the medical stuff, and after you get a chance to read them, I'll sign them."

However, my fever was so high, my vision was blurry. I could only read the headings. I flipped through the pages and, in spite of being unable to focus well enough to read most of it, I did recognize standard forms.

"You can sign these. They won't do your surgery until you do."

Life remained hazy over the next few days. My doctor called to check on me, and change my medication. Adam's doctors called to discuss changes in his condition after his surgery.

Grandma Elena remained the one constant in our lives. She kept the household running. I was so weak, I was sleeping all the time, and my condition continued to deteriorate. Grandma Elena would come into my bedroom and stroke the hair off my face to wake me. Her hand felt cool and soothing on my fevered forehead. She would coax me to eat and drink, but all I wanted was orange juice. She'd bring me cold glasses from the kitchen. She'd get my children off to school and then make sure all the things my children and I needed were done. After she saw us settled in bed for the night she'd return home.

Tuesday, after Adam's surgery, his doctor called and asked me to return to the hospital to discuss the results of Adam's tests, surgery, and his prognosis. Grandma Elena drove me and waited while I went into Adam's room to hear what the doctors had to say. The tests showed none of the usual indicators for heart problems. This left two possibilities — stress, he had a high stress job, and heredity, he had been adopted. Still in a fog, I understood the implication.

"Wow, we have three children."

Adam looked at me and said, "Well, they are stressful, but I don't think they caused this."

"No, not what they did to you, what you did to them — heredity."

Before I left, the doctor pulled me to one side in the hall. "He most likely will have ten relativity healthy years. After that, it will be a crap shoot. You need to be prepared."

No one discussed the depression heart patients often face. I now believe depression started the downward spiral leading to Adam's excessive drinking and death at 57.

The next day my doctor called to report that, since my medication was ineffective, he wanted me in the hospital. He had wanted to wait until Adam's condition improved enough for him to come home. But the timing just wasn't on our side. I remember feeling a sense of relief, knowing I would at last get the medical care I needed.

My children were at school and it would be up to Grandma Elena to explain my disappearance. There wasn't a way to make them feel comfortable with what was happening. They were facing the reality that both their parents were now hospitalized with life threatening conditions.

Grandma Elena was relieved the doctor was admitting me to the hospital. She had been worried that I needed more medical care than could be provided in a home setting. She helped me walk to her car. As I got to the front door, I grabbed the jam and turned to her. "It's all yours. Do whatever you want." I knew how weak and sick I was and I was not sure I would ever return.

Grandma Elena slept at our house and Papa Frank stopped by often to check on how he could help. The laundry pile needed attention, so Grandma Elena started the washer. When she called to say the washer was broken, I told her I knew. "You just put your hands on each side of the agitator and start it. It will work for the whole cycle."

Her reaction was a solid, "No." She had already asked Papa Frank to check it. His solution was to declare it dead and order a new washer.

Neighbors and friends started delivering food. For 45 days, someone provided dinners. Friends and strangers organized prayer chains. It seemed everyone we knew offered to help, except for my mother. Of course, her absence and lack of help was not lost on my son or anyone else.

Grandma Elena brought Ethan to visit me. He had been riding his bike to school without his helmet. When she called to him he ignored her. She decided we needed to talk.

"Oh, Ethan, what do you think you are doing being difficult with Grandma Elena? What do you think will happen if you run her off?"

I knew the chances of him being able to run her off were about as good as his chances of turning off the sun. But I wanted to know his thinking.

His reason shocked me. "Then your mother will come. She can make you well." Although, my mother had been nothing more than a shadow figure in the lives of my children, Ethan knew that she was a Registered Nurse and had spent her career working in the health care industry. From his point of view, things were just getting worse with my hospitalization.

"My mother. Oh, Ethan, my mother isn't coming."

"But if I got sick, you'd come and take care of me."

"Yes, but that is you and me, not my mother."

He was a powerless little boy desperate to change events. I understood his desperation, but I needed to guarantee his cooperation, so I painted the bleakest picture I could.

"Let me tell you what would happen to you and your sisters if we didn't have Grandma Elena. Social Services would come and take you away because children can't stay alone. No one has room for three children, so you'd not be together. You'd be far enough away that you couldn't go to your school or see your friends. When Mommy and Daddy recovered, we couldn't just come and get you. We'd have to go to court and prove we could take care of you before they would release you to us."

I don't know how much of my scenario was true, but it worked. I had also left out the fact several friends had called and offered to take the children to give Grandma Elena a break. Grandma Elena had refused all offers.

When Adam was released five days after his surgery and returned home to continue his recuperation, Grandma Elena went home to sleep for the first time since I had been admitted to the hospital.

My doctor understood the stress our hospitalization was creating for our children. He wanted to send me home as soon as he could. I had improved since being admitted and he ordered a chest x-ray to see if my pneumonia had cleared.

After the x-ray, I crawled into my hospital bed exhausted, and went to sleep. When I woke I knew I was in trouble. I felt as if I had become part of the bed. I reached for the call button.

"How can I help you?" the voice in the wall said.

"Tell the nurse I'm in trouble and to bring her thermometer," I managed to reply.

The nurse was at my bedside moments later, placing a thermometer in my mouth. She didn't wait for the mercury to record my temperature. "I'll be right back with something to help you."

She returned saying, "I talked to the doctor and this will help you." She injected a vile of medicine into the IV line in my arm.

"This better work. There's not much of me left," I said as I watched her work.

"I know. It will. I'll make it work. You should sleep now." The determination in her voice was reassuring.

I had always been a fighter. I had become so weak that much as I wanted to fight, I could feel my body shutting down. I had the will to live but no strength. I slept.

When I woke, I could feel the medicine had been working hard. I was no longer part of the bed but simply lying on it again. I felt stronger. The nurse had been right.

They released me two days after my relapse. Adam and I were amazed at how weak we were. Taking a simple shower, or walking from one room to the next was exhausting. The old saying "as long as you have your health," took on new meaning.

As we grew stronger, Grandma Elena turned over more and more responsibilities to us, but still kept a close eye on everything. We made it through the holidays. Good friends took our children to cut down a Christmas tree. People continued to bring dinner every night. The children went to activities and spent time with friends.

By January, Adam went back to his office part time. In February, my grandmother died. In poor health and in her 90's, we felt she didn't need the worry of knowing about our illnesses. Still the hits kept coming. We were thankful we had Grandma Elena and Papa Frank watching over us.

Many years later, Ethan recalled that time when he wrote Grandma Elena a heartfelt thank you and apology letter. Deep into his addiction and in jail for 30 days, he wanted Grandma Elena to know how much her love and support meant to him.

Day of Terror

The oldest and strongest emotion of mankind is fear,
and the oldest and strongest kind of fear
is fear of the unknown.
—H. P. Lovecraft

The crucible of crisis had brought us closer together. On a late summer Sunday in 1991, the day started as usual. After church, Charlotte and Ethan went to work as lifeguards at the city pool. Megan, almost 13, had decided to "hang out" with a neighbor friend, Lisa. Adam went off to visit Papa Frank. I was refinishing a table for Charlotte to take with her to college. Charlotte called and asked Megan to bring her allergy medicine to the pool. Megan agreed and asked Charlotte if she could ride Charlotte's new bike. The bike didn't fit Megan, since she was 5" shorter than Charlotte — her 1st bad decision. Megan invited her friend Lisa to come with her. Since Lisa didn't have a helmet, Megan decided to leave her helmet on the couch — her 2nd bad decision.

All of a sudden, Lisa appeared on the porch, sobbing. Fighting panic, I said, "Lisa, what's wrong? Where's Megan?"

The answer came between her sobs. "Megan had an accident. So much blood...Mrs. B, so much blood...so much blood."

I ran out in the street. Nothing. I could see nothing. I ran back and took Lisa by the shoulders, and looking into her eyes, my voice sharper than I wanted it to be, I said, "Do you know where she is? Can you take me to her?"

She could only nod.

"Lisa, the best way to help Megan is to direct me to her. Get in my car."

I ran inside to get keys, shoes, and a sheet. What happened? Had a car hit Megan? So much blood. What did she mean? Was she referring to a large gash, an arterial spray? Would Megan bleed to death before I could get there? Would she die in my arms? How long had it been since the accident? Minutes mattered. I had no answers and Lisa was in no condition to give details.

As I backed out of the driveway, Adam came walking up the street.

"Hey, where are you going?"

"Megan's been in an accident. If you want to come, get in."

I'm not sure I brought the car to a full stop, but he managed to climb in the back seat. In full panic mode, I'm issuing orders. I have no time for extra words — no please or thank you. It's not the best part of my personality, but it has always worked well for me in a crisis.

At the first corner, "Lisa, which way?"

"Straight."

At the next corner, "Lisa, which way?"

"Straight."

"I don't see her. How much farther?"

"There, see there."

Megan was sitting cross-legged in the street, next to a man who lived in the house behind the spot where Megan had fallen. He had seen the accident and rushed out to help. Lisa had asked him to stay with Megan while she came for me. As I bolted from the car, I heard the most incredible primal sound. Not a moan, not a scream, but a sound I cannot describe, coming from deep inside Megan, as she rocked back and forth. I ran, calling out to her, but got no response. She didn't turn in my direction. When I got to her, I held her shoulders trying to see into her face. "Megan. Megan. It's me, Mommy."

Megan didn't recognize me. I could have been a tree. She looked past me into another world.

The blood was coming from a one-inch scalp wound that ran down her face. When she wiped it away with her forearms, she smeared it on her face and arms. The man sitting with her said, "I think she chipped her tooth."

I don't know what he saw to make him think that. A week would pass before I remembered his comment and I checked her teeth, but found nothing wrong.

At the scene, I was more concerned about her "chipped brain."

When I looked up, a woman holding a baby had appeared. I looked at Adam and said, "We need to take her."

The woman responded. "You can't take her."

I looked at her and said, "We're her parents and she needs to go to the hospital."

She stepped forward as if to block my path to the car. "I called 911," she insisted.

I looked at Adam and said, "Tell her." I meant for him to ask her to step back, to act as crowd control.

He looked at the woman and simply said, "Oh, I'd step back if I were you."

The woman stared at me in horror and stepped back. I thought that's not exactly what I meant, but it worked.

I gathered Megan in my arms. She weighed about 85 lbs. to my 125 lbs. As I carried her to the car, Lisa opened the door. I backed in, with Megan on my lap.

"Put her feet in," I said to Adam, "and drive."

"To the hospital?" he said.

"Yes, as fast as you can. Don't take any chances. Obey the traffic laws. An accident will only slow us down." I listened. Still no sirens. No one was on the way to help us. We were only about three miles from the hospital.

As the car started to move, I shouted out the window, "Lisa, take the bicycle home." Poor kid, I had nothing for her. She remained terrified. My focus was on Megan.

I pulled Megan to me. Her eyes closed. She had gone somewhere I could not reach. I began to pray. I was begging. "God, don't take her. I can't lose her, not now. Please not now."

The triage nurse saw us pull up and ran out with a wheelchair. We loaded Megan into the chair and were taken into a treatment area. Adam remained in the waiting room. He fainted at the sight of blood, so he took charge of filling out the paperwork.

The first time I gave Adam an update was while the doctor examined Megan. He asked if I needed a change of clothes. The question struck me as odd considering everything else that needed our attention.

Megan still had not spoken, but screamed when the nurses attempted to insert an IV line. The one thing Megan never lacked was fight. The nurses tried to explain what they were doing and why, but the words meant nothing to Megan. All of a sudden, she turned to me. "Go get my mommy. I need my mommy."

"I'm right here, honey."

"Oh." She went back to fighting the nurses. I realized she was only seeing shadows.

After Megan ripped out the first IV and the pressure bandage meant to keep her from bruising, I told the nurse to tie down Megan's free hand.

"You would allow that?" she said.

"Yes, it's the only way she'll leave the IV alone. You don't need to restrain her feet. She's not trying to get off the gurney."

I left to give Adam another update.

This time I found Charlotte and Ethan along with Grandma Elena and Adam in the waiting room.

Charlotte spoke first. "What are they doing to her? I know that's her screaming. I recognize her voice."

I explained about the IV.

Grandma Elena was sitting with her purse on her lap, gripping it with both hands, turning her knuckles white.

I looked at her and said, "It's going to be alright."

"Are you sure?" she said.

"I hope so." I couldn't promise and Grandma Elena knew me so well she could read my thoughts.

Adam again asked if I wanted a change of clothes. I still didn't understand his interest in my clothing. This time I accepted. He asked what I wanted. I thought he needed something to do. I suggested the dress I had worn to church that morning.

The next step in Megan's evaluation was an MRI. As I watched from the doorway, I could see Megan attempt to get off the gurney every time it began to move. I turned to the doctor, "You'll have to sedate her." He responded he had already sedated her as much as he could.

He indicated he had given her enough to bring down a horse and couldn't believe her sustained fighting.

I asked to hold her. I knew I could keep her calm.

He responded that the hospital wouldn't allow it.

Just then the sedation overcame Megan. She remained still for the test, giving me time to make another report to my family in the waiting room.

Lisa and her mom had now joined the family. No one looked comfortable. Adam had my dress. While waiting for the MRI results, I took the dress and went to find a private room so I could change.

An orderly asked if he could help me. He suggested I wait while he found a doctor. I explained I just needed to change my clothes. He pointed around the corner to a bathroom. I was so confused. Why was Adam concerned about what I was wearing? Why had the orderly offered to find a doctor for me?

I closed the door, ran the water and splashed my face. In a crisis, Daddy had always sent me to wash my face saying it would make me feel better. I needed to feel better. I looked into the mirror and recoiled. I had no idea. Blood covered the front of my shirt and was splashed over my neck and jaw. I had held Megan so tight that I was covered in her blood. I collected myself, washed the blood off, threw away the shirt and slipped into the dress.

I finished just as the doctor arrived with the MRI results. He could move Megan to a treatment room and stitch her scalp. I went to the waiting room and shared the good news.

"You can all go home. I'll bring Megan home as soon as they finish stitching her scalp."

I could tell Grandma Elena was not going to leave, so I asked her to drive us home.

In the treatment room, Megan began to repeat, "Call nine one one. I need help. Call nine one one. I need help. Call nine one one. I need help. Call nine one one. I need help."

"We are nine one one."

"Oh" she said, and went back to her mantra.

I turned to the nurse, "Maybe I drilled that in a little too deep." She smiled and nodded.

By the time the doctor finished stitching Megan's scalp, she had begun to have moments of clarity and her vision was starting to return. Armed with instructions for Megan's care, I was able to take her home. Grandma Elena drove and helped me settle Megan in my bed. Megan and I were together day and night for the next week. Every two hours — day and night over the next two days — Megan woke up and we had the same conversation.

"Why am I in your room?"

"You fell off your bicycle and hit your head."

"No, I didn't."

Taking her hand, I guided it to her head where she could feel the small cut.

"What's that?"

"That's where you hit your head."

I knew I had to get the blood out of Megan's hair to prevent it from matting. Grandma Elena came over to help. We used towels to pad the top of the washer and dryer. Grandma Elena brought a short hose with a shower attachment she used to wash her hair in her garage laundry sink. We laid Megan on the towels with her head over the sink as I washed her hair. The water ran red, then pink and finally it ran clear. Grandma Elena held Megan and spoke to her, as she stroked her arm. We wrapped her hair in a towel and took her back to bed.

Over the next couple of weeks, Megan recovered, but remained on restricted activity for a couple of months. Grandma Elena came over each day to check on Megan. Her visits gave us a chance to decompress. We reassured and comforted each other. We drank coffee and talked about how frightening the accident had been. Megan had almost missed out on the first days of high school and the rest of her life.

Storm Clouds Form

A son is a son till he takes him a wife,
a daughter is a daughter all of her life.
—Irish Saying

Storm clouds between Grandma Elena and Doris gathered from their first meeting and continued to grow over the years. Ralph brought Doris, his future wife, home to meet his parents, but the introduction didn't go as planned.

Grandma Elena was put off when she learned her daughter-in-law to be, was studying to become a flight attendant not an aeronautical engineer as she claimed. Grandma Elena had trained to fly small private planes in her youth. Unable to overcome her motion sickness, she had given up her goal to become a pilot. She had a great respect for engineers and pilots.

Wedding planning added stress to their already strained relationship. Ralph and his brother Gene were very different individuals. They didn't get along. Ralph became angry when Grandma Elena insisted he ask Gene to be his best man. She also insisted Ralph let Gene set up the sound system at the reception. The controversy showed the discrepancy between the way things stood and Grandma Elena's perception of how things should appear. She felt the brothers should get along and like each other. However, that didn't reflect the brothers' actual relationship. At first, I thought different interests caused the discord, but it ran much deeper. The inability to accept the current reality, rather than how she wanted the relationship to be, became a major problem for Grandma Elena in her later years. I thought the wedding skirmish would blow over.

Since Grandma Elena grew up during the Great Depression and was not able to go to college, she couldn't understand why anyone given the opportunity, would not continue their education. When Doris dropped out of college, Grandma Elena made her disapproval known.

I observed that Ralph had a tendency to complain about his wife to Grandma Elena. I was sitting one morning with Grandma Elena in the kitchen when Ralph stopped by. He said he wanted to hang out for a while because he and Doris had been arguing. According to Ralph, Doris was complaining about ironing 14 shirts. Ralph had asked what she did all day. He pointed out that he only wore one shirt a day, so she had not ironed for two weeks.

I couldn't help but think how upset I would be with my husband if he complained to his mother about me. I kept thinking Ralph should talk to Doris and not to his mother. As she would over the next few years, Grandma Elena sided with Ralph. I know it's hard not to take your child's side, but it would have been much smarter for Grandma Elena to stay out of that mine field. Even better, she could have helped her son understand his wife's point of view.

When Ralph's complaints pitted Grandma Elena and Doris against each other, he had the two most important women in his life fighting over him. The power struggle between Grandma Elena and Ralph, Doris, and later their daughters, continue to escalate.

Once Ralph and Doris decided to start a family, Doris indicated she was using the same doctor Grandma Elena had used for her surgery years earlier. That announcement appalled Grandma Elena. She told Doris about the mistake the doctor had made and suggested she find a different doctor. I believe Grandma Elena's motive was to protect Doris. She feared her former doctor might make another mistake. It soon became a power struggle. Doris remained committed to her decision, refusing to change doctors.

After Sandra, Ralph, and Doris' first daughter was born, a period of relative peace reigned, but it didn't last long. In place of building a loving relationship, where both sides gained, Ralph, his family, and Grandma Elena's relationship deteriorated which created pain and loss.

Doris and Grandma Elena had very different parenting styles. Grandma Elena often disagreed with Doris' approach.

Doris once complained to Grandma Elena about Sandra, now pre-school age, breaking an expensive crystal bowl. According to Doris, Sandra got up after Ralph left for work and before Doris was out of bed. Alone in the kitchen, Sandra began looking for something to eat. She attempted to take a crystal bowl out of the refrigerator and dropped it.

Grandma Elena believed Doris should have gotten up when her daughter woke up and prepared a breakfast for her. As the conversation between Grandma Elena and Doris continued, Doris admitted Sandra often got up and attempted to find something to eat. She had broken other dishes.

When Grandma Elena retold the story to me, I attempted to defend Doris. Children sometimes get into things. You can't always stop them, I told her. But Grandma Elena would not countenance any excuses for Doris. She countered, "Have your children ever broken something or gotten into food because they were hungry and up alone?"

"No."

My children often made their own breakfast as they got older. I believed everyone should learn to cook starting with breakfast, an easy meal.

The relationship between Doris and Grandma Elena continued to deteriorate. Grandma Elena's dislike of Doris was shared and supported by Papa Frank. A quiet man, he avoided disagreements with Doris. And yet, he surprised me one afternoon when I wandered in looking for Grandma Elena and found Papa Frank sitting on the patio. He looked up and said, "I can't stand that woman."

"Who Papa Frank?"

"Ralph's wife."

I was dumbfounded. "What happened?"

"Nothing, I just can't stand her. If I were Ralph, I'd leave. I don't know why he puts up with her, but that's Ralph's problem. Now, my other daughter-in-law Gene's wife, she's a doll. I think she's great."

I was so shocked. "I really don't know what to say."

He shook his head, "Nothing to say."

Papa Frank didn't say much, but when he did he had strong opinions.

As Sandra got older, she fell in love with ice skating. Doris made Sandra's costumes. She even learned to sew some of the most difficult fabrics, in my opinion, and produced beautiful costumes. Grandma Elena admired Doris' handwork.

Doris believed Sandra had great potential as an Olympic skater, and yet, Ralph was not convinced. When Doris and Sandra wanted to buy expensive professional skates, Ralph asked Grandma Elena for her opinion of Sandra's potential.

Grandma Elena believed Sandra did not have the grace or poise to advance past the local competitions. She told me Sandra looked awkward on the ice and she felt almost embarrassed for her. Grandma Elena felt encouraging Sandra to continue to compete would result in disappointment. Grandma Elena suggested Sandra should pursue something else, where she would have a better chance to succeed, if competing was important to her.

Grandma Elena informed Ralph, "Allowing Sandra to continue would be a waste of money. You might as well pile the money in the street and set it on fire."

The next time Grandma Elena saw Sandra, the youngster was beside herself with joy over her new expensive professional skates. Grandma Elena later asked Ralph, "Why did you agreed to buy the skates?"

He responded, "Mom, I get tired of sleeping on the couch."

A short time later, Sandra quit skating. I always wondered what was lost and why. There seemed to be a real connection between Doris and Sandra and her skating. Doris received positive feedback about the beautiful costumes she made, while Sandra liked the physical activity. Plus, Sandra had made friends with the other skaters.

I wondered how important it was to make a name in skating or if the focus should have been on a little girl having fun.

Out and out war between Doris and Grandma Elena raged. As a result, Ralph and his family spent less and less time visiting. When they decided to move to Tennessee, the separation became more profound.

Grandma Elena and Ralph's problems, over the last 40+ years may be unique in detail, but the fact remained their relationship evolved and changed. Like many people, they drifted apart. Being related by blood and marriage did not foster a closer and closer bond. The way Grandma Elena envisioned the end of her life, including the people supporting her, did not take into account the changes in her relationships and economic realities. What was true in her 60's was completely different from the realities she faced in her 90's.

The war between Grandma Elena and Doris had expanded to include Doris' daughters. While living in Tennessee, Sandra, Cynthia, and Sandra's less than one-year-old-son, Zander, came to visit Grandma Elena and Papa Frank. That visit ended in a major confrontation. The girls and baby had come to visit at meal time. Although Grandma Elena offered to prepare Zander's food first, Cynthia began to feed him grapes from a bowl on the table. Grandma Elena objected to feeding grapes to the baby. She argued that Cynthia needed to cut them in half to prevent Zander from choking. Cynthia later claimed she had cut the grapes.

Sandra and Cynthia began shouting at Grandma Elena, objecting to what they felt was interference. Papa Frank, using a walker, entered the kitchen and ordered, "Everyone get out." He wouldn't tolerate anyone speaking with disrespect to his wife in his home. He kept yelling at them to "get out" until they grabbed their things and left.

I cannot imagine my grandfather telling a grandchild to get out. Nor could I imagine myself or any of my cousins speaking in a disrespectful manner to our grandparents, parents, aunts, uncles or any adult relative. Although my mother and I didn't get along and our world views were different, I addressed her with respect.

Sandra and Cynthia's attitude toward Grandma Elena contrasted with the attitude expressed by my children.

Instead of conflict, my children and Grandma Elena sought out the company of each other.

My children found it easy to be respectful of Grandma Elena and Papa Frank with never a cross word.

In the eighth grade, Charlotte wanted to have a more consistent source of spending money than babysitting provided, so she began delivering newspapers in our neighborhood. Grandma Elena invited her to have breakfast on the weekends. "Your family is still asleep when you finish, so come here and have breakfast with us. We can have a nice visit."

Years later, when Ethan was attending community college, he didn't like going home to an empty house for lunch. Instead he would go to Grandma Elena's house. She welcomed him and even bought his favorite sandwich meats.

"Grandma Elena, he can go home for lunch," I reminded her.

"Yes, but then I wouldn't have a nice visit with him every day. He tells stories that make me laugh. We have a good time," she replied.

"Fair enough. I'll stay out of it."

Losing Papa Frank

A grandfather is someone with
silver in his hair
and gold in his heart.
—Anonymous

By 2001, Papa Frank began to decline. I found it painful to watch, like seeing my own father's decline. Grandma Elena served as Papa Frank's sole caregiver. She refused help, insisting she could cope. It took a physical and mental toll on her, but she would not give up or give in.

Since Ralph, and his family were living in Tennessee, they made few visits. During one visit to California, I told Ralph that Papa Frank's health was failing and I expressed my concerns about Grandma Elena. As everyone focuses on the patient, the needs of the caregiver are often ignored. I could see how she tired. I talked to her about bringing someone in to assist with Papa Frank. I thought she needed relief a couple of hours a day. Grandma Elena refused.

She said, "I don't want to use our savings for Papa Frank's care if it can be avoided. I'm concerned I'll need the savings for my own care someday."

I'd never talked to Grandma Elena or Papa Frank about their finances, so I didn't know their situation. I thought Ralph would know more about the possibility of paying for a caregiver. I wanted Ralph to join me in talking to her about getting help a couple of hours a day.

"I'm not getting involved unless I walk in and find a puddle of urine on the floor, and then I'll send everybody to a home," Ralph said without feeling.

His thoughtless response hit me like a punch in the gut.

As the years went by, Papa Frank became sicker and less mobile, so he began to use a walker, making the front steps unsafe. Charlotte, and her husband, Paco, designed and built a ramp so Papa Frank could access the car.

Papa Frank was too sick the day of Megan and Jim's wedding to attend. Although they were heart sick to miss the ceremony Grandma Elena wouldn't leave him in someone else's care.

Megan and Jim were on their way to their reception, when they detoured to share a few moments with Megan's grandparents. As bride and groom, their special day would not be complete without including Grandma Elena and Papa Frank.

By October, Papa Frank had been hospitalized. Charlotte, Megan, and I met Grandma Elena at the hospital in time to hear the doctor's prognosis. As the doctor sat on one side of the bed, Grandma Elena, Charlotte, Megan, and I surrounded the other sides as he reviewed Papa Frank's test results. No treatment option was left other than keeping Papa Frank comfortable the doctor reported. Grandma Elena wanted to fight his condition. She demanded a cure. Papa Frank sat up, looked straight at her and said, "Mama, I know this is not what you want, but it would be a miracle if I were alive at Christmas."

All the oxygen left the room.

Megan, standing next to me, gulped down a sob. I put my arm around her shoulder and guided her out the door into the arms of a passing nurse. I went back to rescue Grandma Elena, who was now looking pale and distressed. I beckoned to her and ushered her out the door. The nurse looked up and turned Megan to face Grandma Elena. They hugged and cried.

With the nurse watching over them, I returned to the room. Papa Frank looked bewildered. He spoke to Charlotte.

"What's the problem? I'm just telling the truth."

Charlotte responded, "Papa Frank, we love you and want you here so we can visit you."

He shook his head. "Honey, I would love to stay and see your babies, but I just can't."

The doctor suggested Papa Frank rest. We took the opportunity to sit in the waiting room and assist Grandma Elena in filling out forms for care options.

At home, I touched Grandma Elena's arm to get her attention. "You must prepare yourself."

She objected, still wanting to fight Papa Frank's condition. "You don't know what a fighter he is. You weren't in Panama when he was burned and almost died."

I whispered, "That's right. Just remember we all lose the last battle."

She nodded. She heard me. We needed to prepare.

Charlotte was worried Papa Frank would die while she and her husband were in Mexico visiting his family over the Christmas holidays. But, Grandma Elena insisted Charlotte go. Papa Frank died in his sleep on December 19, 2001. Grandma Elena delayed the memorial service until January, after Charlotte and Paco returned. She said it would not be right to have the service without Charlotte.

Grandma Elena invited me to give a eulogy at the memorial service.

> My name is Jo Ann Blum. Harvey James Franklin was my very good friend. Like me, many have known his warm and generous friendship. He was there for me in many ways over the years. He had words of encouragement, and, in my darkest hours, he put his hand on my shoulder. I knew that he thought I would persevere to brighter days, so great was his gift to me.

> I don't know anyone who called him Harvey. Most of us called him Frank. Two of us called him Dad. Some of us called him Chief, but at our house he was called Papa Frank. In the child-speak of our home, Papa Frank was synonymous with Grandfather.

> Grandfather is a word that comes to mean what our experience tells us it means. Some of my greatest childhood pleasures were of being spoiled by my grandfather. When my children Charlotte, Ethan, and Megan were very young, my father died. No small part of that loss was the void he left where a grandfather should be. I feared that my children had lost the chance to have the same positive grandfather experiences that I had had. Papa Frank became their grandfather, obligated only by love. No greater bond was ever made.

Papa Frank was the giver of cookies and sometimes candy. He let you play in his boat, listened to your stories and songs, and watched you dance. He was patient and kind and could repair broken toys. One day he saved 4-year-old Ethan from a horrible fate. Ethan was to accompany Grandma Elena, his two sisters, and me on an all-day outing to fabric stores. Papa Frank insisted that Ethan be left behind. They would spend the day together in the garage. They did.

When we returned at dinnertime, the two were still in the garage sitting surrounded by nuts and bolts — fasteners. There were different kinds of fasteners that needed to be sorted into separate bins. At dinner, Ethan explained, among other things, the difference between a wood screw and a sheet metal screw. "People need to know this to sort them, and they need to be separated because they are used for different things."

Who else would teach this to a four year old? Papa Frank wrote his own definition of grandfather.

On a Friday afternoon in October, Papa Frank was in the hospital. He had been dozing all day. Grandma Elena and I were there waiting for the doctor. As I watched down the hall from the door of Papa Frank's room, I spied not the doctor but my daughters, Charlotte and Megan. They'd taken the day off from their jobs and had arrived for the weekend. The girls greeted us and I encouraged them to go in and wake Papa Frank. As they stood at the foot of the bed and spoke, he roused a little. It didn't take long for him to identify those two young, professional women. More awake than he had been all day, he exclaimed with pride, "There they are...my cookie crunchers."

The wife of the patient in the next bed turned and asked, "Are these young ladies your granddaughters?"

"Yes, they are."

No matter how grown they became, in Papa Frank's heart, Charlotte, Ethan, and Megan were as they were when the world had no cares. And Megan could climb in his lap to read him a story from her picture book. Or when Ethan sat at his feet and showed him the wonder of a new toy from Christmas morning. Or when Charlotte held his index finger because her hand was too small to hold his hand and led him around Ralph and Doris' wedding reception.

It is a circle of love unbroken. No more obvious than in the nursing home as Grandma Elena, Ethan, Charlotte, her husband Paco, and Megan and her husband Jim, stood around Papa Frank's bed. He began to refer to the measure of a circle, and when asked what kind of circle, he said, "A circle like this one, a circle of family."

So, I propose to you, that Papa Frank would want to be remembered by that love.

Love Doesn't Die

Now that I have died
If you need to weep
Cry for your brother
Walking the street beside you.
And when you need me
Put your arms around anyone
And give them what you need to give me.

I want to leave you something
Something better than words or sounds.

Look for me in the people I've known and loved
And if you cannot give me away
At least let me live in your eyes
And not on your mind.

You can love me most by letting hands touch hands
By letting bodies touch bodies
And by letting go of children
Who need to be free.

Love doesn't die.
People do.
So now when all that's left of me is love
Give me away.

—Author Unknown

Different Views of Home

What strange creatures brothers are!
—Jane Austen

Both Gene and Ralph had married women named Doris. Despite having the same name, those women could not have been more different. Grandma Elena and Papa Frank adored Gene's wife. It was a sad day when Gene's young wife died from cancer. She was a loving person, engaging, well-read, and knowledgeable on many subjects, and she was a great storyteller. A light went out for all of us when she passed. I believe Gene never recovered from the loss.

Not long after his wife's death, Gene was debilitated by several strokes. As a result, he could no longer work or live alone. So, the decision was made to move him in with Grandma Elena. Her sewing room once again became Gene's bedroom. Charlotte, Paco, and Ralph painted the room and laid new carpet so Gene's furniture could be brought in to a fresh attractive room. He lived with Grandma Elena from 2006 until he was admitted to the Veterans Home four years later.

Grandma Elena, then 84, loved having her oldest son living with her. They were great companions. But the hard work of caring for him was taxing since Gene suffered short term memory loss. Ralph was the one who secured a place for his brother in the Veterans Home. That meant Grandma Elena no longer had the day-to-day responsibilities of his care. Knowing Gene was well cared for in the Veterans Home did not stop Grandma Elena from missing him. At first, she blamed herself for being unable to care for his physical needs. In time, she came to terms with the fact that Gene was happy, safe, secure, and no longer dependent on her. The difference in Grandma Elena's relationships with her two sons was never more obvious than during that time. Even as he worked for Gene's benefit, Ralph's comments made it clear he resented the excellent relationship Gene and his mother had. Ralph's relationship with his mother continued to deteriorate.

Grandma Elena complained often about Ralph and his disdain for his brother. Ralph later claimed his mother resented him for making the arrangements for Gene to go to the Veterans Home. He argued that she felt he had taken Gene away from her. From my perspective, his claim was untrue. Grandma Elena praised Ralph for making the arrangements and appreciated knowing Gene would be secure.

Ralph would sometimes take Gene to visit Grandma Elena. Those visits would last several days, which meant Grandma Elena would have to prepare meals, make sure Gene took his medicine, and look after his general needs.

On a Monday in November, 2011, Ralph took Gene back to the Veteran's Home, cutting short his stay with Grandma Elena by two days. She became very upset, saying Ralph was punishing her. I asked Ralph, "Why have you cut the visit short."

He told me, "After Gene had a toilet accident in the night, Grandma Elena had called asking for help to get things cleaned up and get Gene back in bed." Ralph became very angry about the late-night call and argued that Grandma Elena could no longer take care of Gene.

Ralph's family made a few visits to Grandma Elena's house. When Ralph visited he brought his grandson, Zander, to see Grandma Elena. However Zander's visits stopped after a big blow up with Sandra and Doris.

Charlotte and her family were visiting with Grandma Elena one Saturday when Ralph and Doris brought Sandra and Zander over. Paco, Javier, age four and one half, and Ralph and Zander, age six and one half, were in the backyard playing. Grandma Elena, Doris, and Sandra were in the living room. Charlotte had taken Ana age two, down the hall to the bathroom. The women heard Ralph yell, followed by Javier's cries. Charlotte looked out the bedroom window to see Paco comforting Javier, who had become frightened by Ralph's loud voice. Doris was told Ralph yelled to stop Javier from throwing a lemon across the yard and over the nine-foot fence into the neighbor's pool. Throwing a lemon that far was an incredible feat for a small child.

When Doris explained to the women in the house why Ralph had yelled, Sandra commented that Ralph did not know how to talk to children. Doris and Sandra then began to discuss Ralph's shortcomings.

Grandma Elena felt, she should defend Ralph. Addressing Sandra, she said, "He is a better man than any man you have had."

Sandra began yelling at Grandma Elena saying she was not going to be called a whore ever again, adding that Grandma Elena could not refer to her son as illegitimate. Grandma Elena had never said either of those things.

The men outside could hear the yelling. As Ralph reached for the sliding glass door, Doris locked it. Charlotte remained in the back of the house because she was unwilling to take Ana into the middle of a very loud argument.

Paco thought the argument was between Sandra and Doris since they were now both yelling. The raised voices had frightened Javier, so Paco had his hands full keeping Javier calm.

Sandra leaned over Grandma Elena, who was sitting in a chair, and shouted at her, causing spit to land on Grandma Elena's face. Sandra then stomped out the front door and headed for the car. Doris followed, but on the way stopped in front of Grandma Elena, to add a few more words of condemnation. Ralph followed with Zander. When Charlotte could no longer hear loud angry voices, she returned to the living room to check on Grandma Elena and share with Paco the details of the argument she'd just heard.

After the argument, Ralph stopped bringing Zander to visit, claiming it was because Zander liked to put puzzles together with the picture face down. Nor did he assemble them from the edges in. When Grandma Elena saw what Zander was doing, she tried to show him an easier way to put the puzzle together.

Ralph claimed Grandma Elena's method was stifling. The explanation seems weak since it came after Sandra blew up at Grandma Elena. Sandra only saw Grandma Elena one more time. That visit also ended with Sandra shouting at Grandma Elena. On that occasion, Grandma Elena's housekeeper was present and ran to get a neighbor to intervene.

I couldn't understand Ralph and Doris' attitude. Grandma Elena taught my children all kinds of things, including how to put a puzzle together, spin a top, and play various games. Her playfulness and desire to teach skills to children seemed loving and kind, the exact opposite of stifling.

How we are perceived by others is important. It can have an influence on how they treat us in our declining years.

Downward Spiral

Sometimes something catastrophic can occur in a split second that changes a person's life forever; other times one minor incident can lead to another and then another and another, eventually setting off just as big a change in a body's life.
—Jeannette Walls, *Half Broke Horses*

The events that led to Ralph having Grandma Elena conserved began with a fall she had late in April 2012. Determined to take her trash bin to the street, she lost control of the heavy bin as it crossed the buckled, uneven cement walk. The gardeners across the street saw her fall and ran over to assist her into her house. She was shaken and bruised. Toward evening, she began to fear she had a broken bone. She called Ralph to take her to the emergency room to be examined.

Grandma Elena often claimed, "If I fall, Ralph will put me in a home. He wants my house."

Nevertheless, one afternoon before trash day, Grandma Elena in her stubbornness attempted to take out the large bin. Ralph had told her he'd stop by in the morning to take out the bin. Perhaps she was angry that Ralph was not being as attentive as she wanted. A long-standing power struggle continued between the two, feeding her fear that she was losing her independence.

As she aged, Grandma Elena had an obligation to herself not to attempt to do things that might result in self-injury. In other words, she needed to be careful and not have unreasonable expectations.

Grandma Elena stopped driving when the Peripheral Neuropathy she developed made it hard to move her legs. She had started to walk by taking slow steps and feared she could not reach the brake pedal in an emergency. Still, she found it hard to adjust to the loss of independence when she quit driving. Since she gave her car to Ralph, she expected him to run errands for her, but that was an unrealistic expectation.

Grandma Elena depended on her neighbor, Clara, across the street to take her to appointments and grocery shopping. She paid Clara for her time.

I tried talking to Ralph and Grandma Elena about managing their expectations of each other. I recommended Ralph sit down with his mother to set up a schedule and explain to her he had family obligations to honor. Ralph refused to do that. As she became more demanding, Ralph's resentment grew more obvious.

It was disheartening for Grandma Elena. She grew up in West Virginia in a large family. When her blind, widowed grandmother needed assistance, her parents, with their children, had spent years caring for the grandmother, living together in the grandmother's house until her death. Grandma Elena was practical enough to realize it would never work for Ralph and his family to live in the same house with her. And yet, the reality did not stop her from wishing for the impossible.

I don't know if Ralph ever wanted to meet Grandma Elena's expectations. However, other pressures appeared to prevent it, including family obligations, health, and his job. Grandma Elena's relationship with other family members played a huge role in Ralph's ability to assist her. Grandma Elena did not think about Doris, Sandra, and Cynthia and the pressure on Ralph when he spent time taking care of her. She also did not take into account the impact his spouse had on his attitude toward her. For almost 40 years, Doris had made her case to Ralph about how she felt about Grandma Elena. That influence on Ralph should not have been discounted. With tension between Grandma Elena and Doris, Ralph was put in an awkward position. Hostilities escalated.

My daughters and I tried to talk to Grandma Elena about making plans for the future. We invited her to come live with us in one of our homes, or buy a house nearby.

Grandma Elena refused our offers. She wanted to stay in her house. It dominated her priorities. She didn't create a clear workable plan acceptable to all parties — a huge mistake. She shouldn't have assumed everyone had the same understanding of their role without proper communication. Circumstances changed, needs changed. Adjustments were required to keep things working well. Everyone had a responsibility to keep the lines of communication open to avoid more bad feelings and misunderstandings.

Grandma Elena ignored the bad feelings she and Ralph shared. She had complained for more than 20 years she could not talk to Ralph.

To understand how bad the communication was between Ralph and Grandma Elena, a portion of Ralph's deposition follows. My attorney, Clarence Brown, is referring to a letter Grandma Elena wrote to Ralph in July 2012, during the conservatorship hearings.

RALPH'S DEPOSITION UNDER OATH IN AUGUST 2015

CLARENCE: ...in the second paragraph, she wrote, "And you don't want to face or discuss our issues, exclamation point, exclamation point, close quote. Is that a true or false statement?

RALPH: In her mind, that was confabulated response. Yes, it's true.

CLARENCE: Okay. You did want to discuss your issues?

RALPH: Why? I might as well pee under the wind because

CLARENCE: Into the wind, do you mean?

RALPH: I'm sorry.

CLARENCE: It's all right.

RALPH: Arguing with my mother is like trying to give an enema to an elephant.

CLARENCE: Okay. So, you —

RALPH: You're not — you're not going to win. So why have the argument?

CLARENCE: So —

RALPH: Why have the discussion? No. I — I need to make a point here. You don't understand my mother. You never will understand my mother. I don't understand my mother.

It's her way or the highway. And this is what she says. When we tried to discuss something with her, it's her confabulated idea of what the world is about and as she perceives it. If you argue, she goes into a screaming match or yelling match because I will sit there and confront her with reality. And she will not accept reality. She never has.

CLARENCE: She never accepted reality?

RALPH: I have never — she has never accepted reality when it comes to her and I discussing the subject.

Grandma Elena and Ralph's inability to communicate was harmful when they tried to organize day-to-day responsibilities, and Ralph tried to take control of Grandma Elena's end-of-life-care and her estate. When Ralph described all communication with her as an argument equal to "trying to give an enema to an elephant," that was not someone she wanted in charge of any aspect of her life.

Grandma Elena and Papa Frank did not review their estate plan after 1990. When Papa Frank died in 2001, some modifications were made to the estate plan to reflect the fact he had died. In February 2007, she asked her attorney to create a new Power of Attorney to remove Gene. This document named Ralph and my daughter Megan, now an adult. Grandma Elena's attorney had moved his office about an hour's drive from her home. She needed an attorney with offices close to her home and easy to reach. She found it hard to access services from an attorney far away. To my knowledge, at no time did Grandma Elena consider not being able to work with the people she had designated to take care of each aspect of her estate. Grandma Elena should have reviewed the choices she had made. That was a critical mistake, in light of the current state of her relationship with Ralph and his family.

In Grandma Elena's case, the focus was on the contentious relationship between Ralph and his family. But no one's life is static. While Ralph lived in Tennessee, he had moved too far away and could no longer fulfill the obligations he agreed to perform. Other obligations interfered after he moved his family back. That made a review of plans essential. A full review with her attorney was critical to be successful in controlling how her affairs were handled when she was no longer capable. She should not have been afraid to ask the people she expected to take on responsibilities when she needed them, "Can you still do this when the time comes?"

On the other hand, Ralph should not have been afraid to respond, "I love you, but I won't be able to take on these responsibilities."

I found it hard to say why Grandma Elena chose to move the bin that led to her fall. That fall set into motion forces that would open the door to removing her from her home.

Grandma Elena had had the same doctor for a long time. However, she hadn't seen him for about two years, by his estimate. Her health was good and she required no medication except for a vitamin B12 shot she received at regular intervals.

After the fall, her doctor expressed concern that the combination of her age and living alone compromised her safety. He recommended that Pathways Home Health and Hospice Services evaluate her living conditions. Pathways staff visited her and noted how well she was coping between April and June 2012. The stated goal was to minimize or eliminate future falls.

In May, Pathways Home Health and Hospice Services report noted:

> ...Ralph was very grateful for the OT's [Occupational Therapist] call; he expressed his exasperation with pt. [patient]. He told the OT "she has alienated everyone but himself and two friends, one of whom he does not trust." He spoke at length re the pt's "need to control" and her refusal to allow him to change tablecloth on dining table, which had not been removed in three years, or to change her sheets. He desires to have conservatorship of pt. The OT concurred with the pt's need for a 24-hr supervised environment, and stated she will communicate same to her Dr. Smith."

If that was what Ralph was telling the caretakers, then he was making gross exaggerations. In fact, neighbors checked on her all the time.

Grandma Elena had not alienated them.

I had changed the tablecloth a short time before that report.

Grandma Elena may not have let Ralph change her sheets, but she did have a housekeeper who changed them. I saw the sheets hanging on the line on many occasions. Because Ralph was her son, and she didn't make it clear she did not want him involved, health care professionals consulted with him.

After Ralph indicated he wanted to have someone come in every day to help Grandma Elena, I arranged for a meeting with two caregivers at Ralph's home to hear what they recommended. I hoped the fact-finding meeting would reveal more options to allow her to stay in her home. The caregivers emphasized the importance of allowing the elderly to continue doing tasks they were capable of handling, assisting only where necessary. Their experience emphasized that people remained happier and healthier the longer they continued to care for themselves.

Ralph called me to announce he had set up an appointment with Dr. Smith, Grandma Elena's doctor, to discuss the results of the home study and wanted me to attend. As we sat waiting to talk to the doctor, Doris, in a snide tone said, "Elena doesn't know anything about medicine."

"What makes you say that?" I said.

"Remember how Elena did not want me to go to the same doctor she had for her surgery? She didn't like him and blamed him for the mistake in her medication and here I have two healthy daughters to prove he is a good doctor."

"Doris, you didn't have any complications with your pregnancies or deliveries," I reminded her.

"See, Elena didn't know what she was talking about."

I saw no point in continuing with that line of reasoning. Still, I thought, if you have no complications, you don't need a doctor. Women have been giving birth to healthy babies for centuries. It's when there's a problem that a doctor is needed. If a mistake is made, it can have devastating, long-lasting consequences. Grandma Elena wasn't wrong. Doris was fortunate to have had a different experience. The conversation reflected a lack of openness and understanding of different points of view that made those family communications almost impossible.

Doris seemed to imply Grandma Elena had no right to her opinion. I saw that attitude over and over as Doris and Ralph referred to choices Grandma Elena made.

Ralph added that Grandma Elena was wrong to ask him to buy personal feminine items when he shopped for her. After a good laugh at Grandma Elena's expense, he brought up the belief Grandma Elena held that Doris controlled him by withholding sex. Again, they laughed.

I was sickened by the conversation. If Ralph was unwilling to take his mother to the grocery store, why then was it inappropriate to ask him to buy personal hygiene items? And if he didn't want his mother to believe he was being controlled by his wife withholding sex, then he should not have complained to her about being tired of sleeping on the couch.

When Dr. Smith came in, he indicated he wanted to see Grandma Elena before he could make a recommendation. In his opinion, old people did better in retirement homes. He indicated the area had many nice retirement homes, adding he thought that was the best alternative for his older patients.

Grandma Elena's doctor indicated he believed a son should be in control of his mother's care. This was not what Grandma Elena wanted. I'm sure the doctor's philosophy worked for some and I believe he had his patient's best interest at heart. However, Grandma Elena never shared her vision of her end of life care. Again, communication was the key to ensuring everyone was in agreement.

Later, Ralph asked Grandma Elena's doctor to fill out a Capacity Declaration in support of his request for conservatorship. Since Grandma Elena had not visited the doctor for over two years, he stated he wanted to see her before he filled out the forms. Ralph made the appointment and drove his mother to the doctor's office. Grandma Elena told Charlotte she knew the purpose of the visit was to have her evaluated. The idea that Ralph requested the evaluation angered Grandma Elena. At the appointment, she sat staring at the floor, refusing to speak. Given her behavior, the doctor agreed her mental capacity had deteriorated and he agreed to sign the requested forms.

Grandma Elena's behavior proved to be her downfall. It didn't matter how angry or insulted she was about Ralph trying to have her evaluated. Her noncompliance supported Ralph's claim that she needed a conservator.

Like many families, my family did not use the courts and the conservatorship laws to protect our older family members. I didn't understand at the time what a conservatorship was and why it would be used.

I had watched my aunt and uncle help my grandmother in her final years. Grandma lived to her mid-90's. She had stopped driving years before and could not have lived in her own home without assistance. Grandma needed help with chores, errands, doctor's appointments, trips to the bank, grocery shopping, and general shopping. I remember Grandma telling me she liked grocery shopping with my aunt. She also appreciated the times when she did not feel good, that my aunt would take her list to the store and buy her groceries. Grandma commented that my aunt knew the brands she liked and was careful to buy what she preferred. This small courtesy reinforced Grandma's independence. It worked because there was communication, love, and respect between Grandma and my aunt and uncle.

Grandma's mind was sharp until the day she died. She had conversations with our family so we knew how she wanted her estate handled. Out of respect and love, her wishes were followed. My grandma was fortunate to have our loving family around her. Sometimes it only takes one person to prevent an estate from being distributed the way the deceased wanted.

The Final Storm

Your pain is the breaking of the shell that encloses you.
—Khalil Gibran

After the blow ups with Sandra, Grandma Elena with great sadness remarked she had written off any hope of having a relationship with that granddaughter. And yet, she held out hope that she and Cynthia, Sandra's younger sister, could form a positive bond.

One May afternoon in 2012, Ralph, Doris, and Cynthia stopped by Grandma Elena's house. She was sitting in her recliner chair when Doris and Cynthia walked in and hovered over her while Ralph stood behind her chair.

Cynthia, who was in her 30's, began by calling Grandma Elena a horrible person and spat out that she had always hated her. Cynthia announced that she wanted to cut Grandma Elena out of her life forever.

Cynthia's words shocked Grandma Elena. She couldn't believe anyone would come into her home and say such terrible things. She looked at Doris, who nodded in agreement with her daughter. She then looked back to see Ralph nodding his head and gesturing for Cynthia to continue.

At this point, Cynthia was standing so close, she prevented Grandma Elena from standing up and leaving the room. To avoid hearing the angry words, she put her fingers in her ears and began to sing "Lalalalala."

After Cynthia finished her tirade, the family walked out. Grandma Elena picked up the phone and called me. She tried to describe the scene, but dissolved into tears. I left my office and drove to her house, where I found her still crying.

Over a cup of tea, Grandma Elena described the scene and Cynthia's statement in detail. I found it difficult to understand what motivated that confrontation. It seemed so cruel. Grandma Elena would turn 90 in a couple of weeks, she no longer drove, and had limited mobility. She certainly had never arrived at Ralph's house unannounced. In fact, she had not gone to Ralph's house for years.

If Doris and Cynthia did not want to have anything to do with Grandma Elena, they could have simply avoided her calls. Phone calls were the only regular contact they had with her. While Ralph had not made it clear where he stood, he had supported Cynthia's stand.

After Grandma Elena calmed down, I went home and called Ralph. He described what happened as Grandma Elena had. He supported Cynthia's statement. Later, Ralph told me Cynthia had felt it necessary to express her feelings because she felt her dad was mistreated by Grandma Elena.

The whole incident caught Grandma Elena by surprise. Before that day, Cynthia had spent a fair amount of time at Grandma Elena's house and she had engaged her in conversation asking about the family history. Cynthia was putting together a family tree. Grandma Elena had hoped those conversations would bring them closer. She told me Cynthia was the one person in Ralph's family who she felt she had a chance with whom to develop a positive relationship.

The summer before, Ralph had brought Cynthia to see Grandma Elena to ask for money so she could pay off her credit cards and enroll in school back East. As far as Grandma Elena knew, Cynthia never enrolled in college. When she could not find a job, Ralph came to Grandma Elena and asked for more money so Cynthia could return to California. The money, free storage of Cynthia's household goods in Grandma Elena's garage, and the time spent discussing family history, had given Grandma Elena hope for a relationship.

After the confrontation, Grandma Elena realized they hated her — dashing her hope for a positive relationship. She began to ask questions. Who would help her? She decided the time had come to change her estate plan and began the process of disinheriting Ralph and his family. With Gene living in the Veterans Home, Grandma Elena believed everything she had would go to Ralph and his family. She was convinced that Gene had everything he needed. So, she began to look at alternatives for her estate distribution.

I knew Ralph's family would not show up to celebrate Grandma Elena's 90th birthday in June 2012, less than a month after their ugly confrontation with Grandma Elena. They had made it clear they wanted nothing to do with her.

As a mother and grandmother, I imagined how painful that ruptured relationship was for all involved. Over the years, Grandma Elena had talked about how important her sons were to her and how proud she was of them. For that important day, neither son would be present to celebrate with her.

My family planned to spend the special day with her. I invited the neighbors to stop by for cake. I arrived mid-morning, and began to set up the food for the party. I bought flowers, snacks, juice, and soda as well as a special cake and deli sandwiches. Megan and Charlotte arrived with their families. They each brought a special gift for Grandma Elena and planned to spend the day with her. Ralph did stop by and brought a card signed by him, only. He stayed no more than ten minutes and refused any offers of food, including cake.

Charlotte and Megan's children played in the back yard. Grandma Elena shared memories and watched a new generation having fun.

The day created special moments for each of us. Ana sang a Perry Como song she learned just for Grandma Elena, "A You're Adorable." Javier described his soccer games and shared the adventure of the book he was reading. Ella performed a special dance. Stephan, the youngest, noticed there were oranges on one of the trees. Grandma Elena told him to pick one. When he stood under the tree showing her he was too short, she told him to use the picker. Stephen, brought an orange and laid it at her feet.

"Pick another," she urged.

From inside the house, I noticed he didn't know how to use the picker. He was catching the end of the branch as well as the orange. I walked up next to Grandma Elena and she pointed at him with great delight, and said, "He's picking oranges."

"Yes," I said, "and he's trimming the tree."

She shooed me away.

"Okay, Grandma Elena, it's your tree."

Stephan picked a dozen oranges while Grandma Elena watched with pride.

Some neighbors came by to wish Grandma Elena a Happy Birthday, and some brought flowers. We had fun watching Grandma Elena surrounded by children. She had such a good time watching the whiffle ball game, listening to the special song and stories, enjoying the dancing, and even picking oranges.

Grandma Elena Sets in Motion New Plans

The best laid schemes o' Mice an' Men,
Gang aft agly [often go awry].
—Robert Burns

Grandma Elena asked me to drive her to the bank so she could remove Ralph's name from her safety deposit box. She said she had been uncomfortable adding him, but he had insisted. Now her fear revolved around concern he would remove the documents she had stored there. The bank's representative told her she would have to close it and open one in her name only. Since the bank did not have one in the size she needed, she removed everything and closed it. The following week we returned to the bank, and she rented a new one.

When Ralph went to the bank to open the safety deposit box, he learned of the change. He then insisted Grandma Elena go with him and put his name back on the box. At the bank, he demanded and argued with Grandma Elena to the point the bank employee became concerned, and filed a possible Financial Elder Abuse Claim with Adult Protective Services.

An investigator from Adult Protective Services contacted Grandma Elena twice after that. She was embarrassed a stranger now knew her son did not respect her and appeared to abuse his access to her finances. She agreed Ralph wanted her money, but having others

know about her situation, made her feel ashamed. We have all heard
the stories of abused wives and children protecting their abusers. Still,
Grandma Elena did not complain to the investigator and did herself no
favor by protecting Ralph. The case was closed as "unfounded" one
month later.

Shortly after her 90th birthday, Grandma Elena began to discuss
leaving her estate to someone else. I insisted she talk to her attorney.

She began referring to Ralph as "Mr. Live, evil spelled
backwards." Their relationship had deteriorated to the point of open
hostility. I kept encouraging Grandma Elena to talk to Ralph. She said
she tried, but after they saw each other, Grandma Elena would
complain, "Mr. Live is snarky and rolls his eyes when I try to talk to
him and then walks away."

One day, when I stopped by at lunchtime, Grandma Elena was
holding papers from her attorney in front of her. As she handed them
to me, she asked, "Would you be willing to do this?" They were Power
of Attorney and Durable Power of Attorney for Health Care
documents. She told me she had explained the situation to her
attorney. Those were the documents he had prepared.

"Does Ralph know what you are doing?"

Grandma Elena responded she did not trust Ralph and believed
Doris controlled him. She kept referring to the argument about
Sandra's skates. The reason he had relented was he was "tired of
sleeping on the couch." That was proof Doris ran their household.
Grandma Elena believed Ralph wanted her house and was afraid he
would "pull the plug" on her if he got the chance. She ended with, "I
need someone I can trust."

I agreed to fulfill the obligations she asked of me. The documents she had were drafts. Since the final documents would need to be signed at the attorney's office, I agreed to drive her to the appointment.

Next, Grandma Elena ordered the Change of Beneficiary forms for her savings accounts and annuity. She asked me to fill in the changes as she directed, saying since I knew addresses it would be easier. She had asked Ralph to do the same thing several years earlier when she named my girls as beneficiaries. The request seemed consistent with past requests. I never imagined anyone would think I had tried to influence Grandma Elena.

In the end, my efforts to help were used to claim I had used "undue influence." To ensure that everyone knew these changes were Grandma Elena's wishes, she should have completed them herself or had her attorney fill them out. After Ralph found the new estate paperwork hidden under Grandma Elena's place mat, he moved into high gear preparing to ask the court for a conservatorship to gain control of Grandma Elena and her assets.

The old 2007 Power of Attorney created a base for Ralph to obtain control through the probate court. The document did not ask for a specialist or any special diagnostic testing. Ralph was given awesome responsibilities contained in a Power of Attorney and Durable Power of Attorney for Health Care documents. As Grandma Elena became uncomfortable with Ralph, it was important she review those documents, especially as her relationship with Ralph had changed.

Grandma Elena had waited too long.

It doesn't make any difference how Ralph found out Grandma Elena had started the process of disinheriting him. It gave him the information he needed to start the conservatorship process, to prevent his disinheritance.

While Ralph collected and prepared the documents he needed to become Grandma Elena's conservator, Grandma Elena and I were busy reviewing her needs.

Grandma Elena said she had always been uncomfortable with Ralph having anything to do with her finances. She felt pressured into letting him help her pay bills. Ralph told the court he had controlled Grandma Elena's finances for the last six years. From Grandma Elena's point of view, they had paid the bills together and she had hoped they could use the time to repair their relationship.

After the confrontation with Cynthia, she felt repair was impossible. I suggested a bookkeeper could come once or twice a month to go over her accounts and pay her bills. I found a woman willing to add a client for about $100 a month. Grandma Elena liked the idea of having professional help with her finances.

Next, we looked for transportation to get her to appointments, and on her errands. She also needed general companionship. Grandma Elena had depended on her neighbor, Clara across the street, and had paid for her time. Hiring a part time caregiver to take over those responsibilities would cost less.

Grandma Elena and I spent each visit discussing options. I wanted to assist her in creating a system of help consistent with her comfort level, and needs.

Friends in the area had recommended three caregivers to me. Grandma Elena asked me to set up interviews. She wanted to be part of the process. Her career hiring for a major corporation would come in handy. I made the initial phone calls to set up the interviews.

During one of my regular lunch hour visits, Grandma Elena showed me a newspaper advertisement for a medical emergency system. It required attaching a wire to a phone jack, and plugging it into an electrical outlet. The person using the system wore a unit with a panic button they could push if they had any type of medical emergency.

I explained she would need a credit card to buy the system. I offered to use mine. To my surprise, she announced she had one. I cannot remember Grandma Elena ever using either a credit card or an ATM card. She always wrote checks, used cash or went inside the bank if she needed anything. She didn't trust computers and that distrust extended to ATMs. When we called the number on the ad, she put the phone on speaker so we could both listen to the sales information. We asked a few questions and the answers satisfied Grandma Elena that the unit was a good idea. The salesman asked Grandma Elena who she wanted the company to notify in case of an emergency.

The emergency system arrived in just a few days. The instructions indicated set up must be completed in a couple of weeks or the unit would not activate. Grandma Elena decided to ask Ralph to install it in the living room. However, the only available phone jack was in the back bedroom and a wire would have to be strung down the hall. Grandma Elena said Ralph and a neighbor boy could string the phone wire under the house. Crawling under the house would require a young person so the neighbor boy sounded like the best option.

A couple of days prior to the deadline, Grandma Elena called to say she was worried. Ralph still had not come over. She was afraid she would miss the deadline to set up the system. I told her my husband, Edward, whom I married in 1998, and I would be back from our weekend getaway on Sunday afternoon. I assured Grandma Elena we would install the unit if Ralph had not done it by then. Ralph later told me he resented that we helped Grandma Elena buy and install the unit.

I felt keeping Grandma Elena involved was important. As people age, the actual loss of control and perceived loss of control are major issues. This played out a few months earlier. The walkways at Grandma Elena's had become trip hazards due to the tree roots lifting the concrete. Grandma Elena agreed they needed to be repaired/replaced. When Ralph brought a contractor to look at the project, he didn't tell Grandma Elena. When she asked what was happening, Ralph told her the purpose of their visit was to get a bid. But he had excluded her in choosing a contractor. Now, he excluded her by deciding the scope and budget for the project. Grandma Elena objected to being left out. It made her feel she was losing control of her property. She became very angry and demanded Ralph and the contractor leave, halting the project.

Ralph Shows His True Colors

How sharper than a serpent's tooth
it is to have a thankless child.
—William Shakespeare

Everything Grandma Elena and I tried to do to organize the support services she needed came to a halt on July 3. Grandma Elena phoned me. Her voice was shaky. "Ralph is suing me."

"I'll come right over." I dropped everything at work and dashed over to find her standing in the kitchen holding a pack of legal papers. Ralph was not suing her. He had served her with papers notifying her of a hearing to establish a conservatorship through the probate court. She had so many questions and I had no answers.

I reminded her, "You have an appointment with your lawyer to sign your updated documents." I had already agreed to drive her to his office. She called Ralph and told him to stay away. She never wanted to see him again. The court papers created a devastating amount of stress for her. Her sense of security evaporated.

In a less hostile relationship, when a conservatorship is used for the right reasons, the advantages could be discussed ahead of the court action. Having a trusted person present when the court papers are delivered would go a long way to limit stress and confusion.

As scheduled, Grandma Elena went to the attorney's office to sign the papers she had asked him to prepare. Grandma Elena and Papa Frank held the common belief that attorneys were expensive so they had limited their contact with them. As a result, they didn't have a close working relationship with their attorney. Their estate documents had become stale.

Ralph's attorney called Grandma Elena's attorney before her appointment to sign the new documents. If Grandma Elena had the established practice of conferencing with her attorney on a regular basis, multiple advantages would have been in place to guarantee her wishes were respected. He felt the best he could do for Grandma Elena was refer her to another attorney closer to where she lived.

As soon as Grandma Elena got home after the signing, she called the recommended attorneys. One attorney didn't answer. The next attorney couldn't see her until Monday.

On Friday, Ralph and his two daughters came to Grandma Elena's house and demanded her checkbooks, credit card, and cash. He had obtained an emergency conservatorship rather than waiting for the scheduled hearing. Ralph and his attorney told the judge they had an imperative need to take control of Grandma Elena's affairs. No notice was given to Grandma Elena. She was not present at the emergency hearing and was not given the opportunity to defend herself. Ralph's move blindsided her.

Grandma Elena ordered Ralph to leave and threatened to call the police. When he didn't leave, she called 9-1-1, and then she called me. When I arrived, Ralph and his daughters were standing outside. The police and Grandma Elena were talking inside. When the police told

Ralph he needed to produce the court order, Ralph sent his daughters home to get it.

Grandma Elena took a lot of convincing to get her to hand over her checkbooks, cash, and credit card. She was humiliated, and felt vulnerable and penniless. I gave her the $20 I had in my wallet. I hoped it would give her a sense of some control. The police understood and treated her with kindness, but they had to obey the court order. They also cautioned her to be nice to Ralph since he now had the power to move her to a care home.

The next day, I saw a post from Cynthia.

She described family as, "My dream world: A world where you choose your family, not your friends, but you are still guaranteed to like your friends. That way you can replace the family members you don't like. If only!!!"

Her older sister, Sandra, hit the like button, on Facebook, indicating her agreement with this definition of family.

I was afraid for Grandma Elena.

On Monday, I took Grandma Elena to see her new attorney, Bob Metcalf. He treated her with kindness and understanding. She told him she was afraid of what Ralph might do since he had his own key to her house. Bob recommended changing the locks. He also advised Grandma Elena to be tested for competence. It would be good evidence to fight the conservatorship. Since Ralph had taken control of Grandma Elena's assets, Bob wrote a check to cover the cost of the testing. It took from July 13 to July 19 for a clinical psychologist to complete the nine hours of testing.

The day after her meeting with the Bob, Grandma Elena called to have the locks changed. She had no money other than the $20 I had given her, so I stopped by to pay the locksmith. When I pulled up, Ralph and a police officer were standing in the side yard. The locksmith was working on the front door, and I could hear the housekeeper vacuuming. A woman I had never seen before was coming out the front door. It looked like a three-ring circus. I worried about what might have happened to Grandma Elena.

As I walked up to the house, the woman introduced herself as the court investigator, Linda Smith, and asked if I would answer some questions. I said I needed to talk with Grandma Elena's attorney first and headed inside.

Cathy, the housekeeper, pulled me to one side as I entered. She urged me to keep Ralph from searching the house. He had already gone through the closets, drawers and cabinets. She thought his actions were upsetting Grandma Elena. Cathy said he had taken things, but she didn't know what things. I found Grandma Elena standing in the corner of the kitchen, looking pale and shaking.

"I'm so glad you're here. I need a friendly face. I feel like an animal trapped in my own kitchen."

I know now, judges depend on the impartial observations of their court investigators. On this day, nothing looked impartial with Ralph and a uniformed police officer standing guard. In my opinion, the court investigator should have assessed the scene and arranged to return on another day to talk with Grandma Elena alone.

Under the intense conditions I witnessed that day, I'm not surprised the court investigator found Grandma Elena confused, forgetful, and unable to answer questions or even explain things in a rational manner. I find chaos disorienting during the best of times.

This is what the investigator wrote. She even misspelled my name.

On July 10, 2012, I made two attempts to visit Elena. On the first attempt in the morning, the drapes were drawn and there was no answer at the door. I was informed that Ralph had arranged for a city police officer to be present for a civil standby later in the day so that Ralph could retrieve financial records. I understand that the police officer had visited just days before when Elena became upset when Ralph tried to visit his mother. After introducing myself and explaining the purpose of my visit, Elena agreed to meet with me in the kitchen. Locksmiths were at the home replacing all door locks. At the end of my visit, the locksmith asked if he should give a key to Ralph. Elena was adamant that a key NOT be given to Ralph.

Elena initially said that she wanted to talk with someone first to make sure she could talk with me. She mentioned her attorney and referred to him as "Bob." I asked if her attorney was Bob Metcalf and Elena said, "Yes." She searched through a note pad on the table looking for his number. Just moments later, Elena asked, "Who was I going to call?" I told her she was looking for Bob Metcalf's number. Again, just moments later, Elena asked who was she going to call and again, I replied that she was looking for Bob Metcalf's number. She dialed a number, asked for Bob, and apparently was told that she had called her clinical psychologist, Dr. Jeffery Harrison. Elena then attempted to find her friend, Jo Anne Blum's ("Jo Anne") number, but could not recall where the number was posted. She searched her message board and then stopped and asked, "Who am I looking for?" Just as before, I replied that she was looking for Jo Anne's number. At one-point Elena quipped, "I guess I'm proving I need help." After several repeats of asking whose number she was looking for and my replying "Jo Anne," Elena agreed to speak with me. I asked Elena who had ordered the services of the locksmith. Elena replied that she had no idea.

The ONLY person present during our meeting was the police officer, who tried his best to calm Elena, who was quite agitated and yelling at Ralph things like, "You just want to take over so you can have my house!" Most of my visit was Elena either looking for a telephone number for Mr. Metcalf, Jo Anne, or yelling at Ralph. At the conclusion of my visit, Elena said she had no idea why Ralph was doing this and that he gets everything when she dies.

Another example of just what an explosive situation this has become, as I was leaving Elena's house, Jo Anne arrived, but declined to speak with me until she had a chance to talk to Elena's attorney. Moments later, Jo Anne handed me her cell phone to speak with Bob Metcalf. I introduced myself to Bob at which point he yelled that Ralph is just "pissed off" because his mother hasn't died so he can have that house. I politely informed Bob that we would talk the next morning as I was wasting the time of a city police officer and had Ralph and Jo Anne standing nearby. My conversation with Bob the next morning was much more civil.

The court investigator should have added that she had returned to visit in the late afternoon. She only made the one contact with Grandma Elena before writing her report. Ralph's earlier visit that she referred to, when Grandma Elena called the police, was the day Ralph had demanded all her checkbooks, cash, and credit card. In Grandma Elena's defense, the investigator's visit came just four days later. No one, including Grandma Elena, knew what the process involved, nor what part each person would play.

Grandma Elena did suffer from some short memory loss, which could become worse at the end of the day, or when she was tired, stressed, angry, and/or scared. Being around Ralph caused her great stress, anger, and fear. A uniformed police officer at Ralph's side only intensified her anxiety.

Megan asked the investigator to visit again earlier in the day so she would see Grandma Elena at a less stressful time. The investigator, however, indicated she did not have time for a second visit.

I cannot blame investigators who have full caseloads, limited time, and too little support. Grandma Elena depended on our court system and expected it to respond to her case with full professional attention. Our judges must demand the finest professional work from their support staff in order to assure the fairest possible ruling.

I am familiar with the process of high quality failure analysis. I have often compared it to CSI without the body and gun. When doing a failure analysis, the engineer interviews the client to learn as much as possible about the conditions at the time of the failure. This information and the initial inspection, point the engineer in a direction to look for the specific cause. As an inspection continues, and test results are compiled, the engineer can confirm the original suspicion or find evidence of a different cause or multiple causes. An open mind is one of the most valuable tools at the engineer's disposal. When compiling observations and test results, inconsistencies cannot be ignored. In fact, they may be what will reveal the true cause of the failure.

When court investigators and attorneys begin to investigate a case for probate court in order to produce a fair result, it's critical to guard against allowing pre-conceived ideas and or past experience to dominate conclusions. When evidence points in different directions, then additional investigations must be done. Just as in failure analysis, some cases are more complex, some have hidden or semi hidden causes, and some take more time to find the root cause. When dealing with people's lives additional investigation is worth the investment.

Based on one visit with Grandma Elena and her interviews with others, the court investigator made a recommendation to the judge.

> During my visit with Elena, she displayed an alarming lack of immediate recall. Her relationship with Ralph has deteriorated to dreadful levels where he is not allowed in the home. I am particularly concerned about Elena's susceptibility. The one person who has unfettered access to Elena openly justifies recent documents signed by Elena while acknowledging that Elena has short term memory

problems that have been reflected in tests. To bring immediate stability and protection to Elena, I respectfully recommend the following:

1) Due to the breakdown in the relationship between Elena and Ralph, that further consideration be given to a neutral third party to serve as conservator on a more permanent basis should there be a need for further conservatorship proceeding. However, to maintain status quo and provide immediate protection, that the temporary conservatorship remain in place;

2) That the court allow Ralph to have a key to Elena's home so that he can gain entry in emergency situations or otherwise to discharge his duties as conservator with appropriate notice;

3) That the court investigators assessment of $600 is due and payable when funds are available.

Before the hearing, Ralph's attorney sent this letter to Grandma Elena's attorney, Bob Metcalf.

We represent Mr. Ralph Franklin as conservator to the person and estate of Elena L. Franklin. Mr. Franklin has a temporary conservatorship and has filed for a permanent conservatorship over Ms. Franklin. Attached as Exhibit A is a copy of the Letters of Conservatorship, issued July 6, 2012. Mr. Franklin is the temporary conservator of the person and estate of Elena Franklin. A hearing is set for July 24, 2012 in Dept. X at the County Superior Court at

1:30 p.m. The hearing will reaffirm the temporary conservatorship until a permanent conservatorship is established.

Ralph's attorney sounded as if he could predict the outcome of the hearing even before any report or test results were available.

The letter continued.

As you are aware, Elena, conservatee, is unable to enter into any contract with any third parties as of the issuance of the Letter of Conservatorship. We have not been advised by your office that you have been retained or represent Ms. Franklin, that any objection have been filed, that your office has been appointed counsel for Ms. Franklin, or any filed notice with the court or court Investigator that you represent Ms. Franklin. Further, you are advised that seeking to represent Elena in this matter requires you to notify our office, the court, and Mr. Franklin, as conservator. Failure to provide proper notice will result in the court's, Mr. Franklin's and our office's spending unnecessary time and effort in ensuring Ms. Franklin's safety.

Ralph and his attorney were clear, they did not want Grandma Elena to have an attorney of her choice. I believe this paragraph implies that Grandma Elena could not retain an attorney without Ralph's permission. Most concerning to me, how does a lack of notification jeopardize Grandma Elena's safety?

Ralph's attorney continued.

We have also been informed by the Court Investigator that you intend to obtain a psychological evaluation of Elena Franklin without a court order or Mr. Franklin's consent. If your office is pursuing this matter on behalf of a third party, we ask that you cease your conduct until the court or our office receives your official appointment as attorney to Elena L. Franklin.

I think they were worried about the test results showing Grandma Elena did not need a conservator. They should have been. Ralph's attorney was just getting warmed up:

Further, we received information that your office has received Elena's modification to her estate plan prepared by Mr. Roy Wilson on Friday, July 6, 2012. If you have information relating to these changes please provide this to our office immediately.

How did Ralph's attorney find out? Where was he getting this information? Or was he just fishing?

He then slammed me with false accusations, misspelling my name.

Finally, our office has received information that Joann Blum is responsible for recent changes in Elena's behavior and to her estate plan. As a party in interest and a party with a conflict of interest we believe that Joann Blum is and has been for the past years financially abusing Elena Franklin for her and her children's benefit. We have recently received information that Elena's credit card was used in Sacramento, CA near to where Joann Blum resides, to purchase products from Sears without Elena being present.

It was so strange to hear Ralph and his attorney claim I was responsible for the changes in Grandma Elena's estate. Ralph and his family were responsible. They had broken Grandma Elena's heart by condemning her character. They were using those changes to her estate plan, and her short-term memory loss, against her. Nor did Grandma Elena help her situation by pretending not to remember whenever Ralph asked her questions. She had discovered it angered and frustrated him, so I believe she used this strategy to upset and divert him. Ralph claimed in court, under oath, he had been taking care of Grandma Elena's accounts for six years. How could anyone financially abuse Grandma Elena if he was overseeing her finances?

Ralph had brought his daughter, Cynthia, to Grandma Elena to ask for several thousand dollars to pay off Cynthia's credit cards. It was Ralph that the bank reported to Adult Protective Services as a possible financial abuser and Ralph used Grandma Elena's credit card to pay for the repair of her refrigerator. Without this background information, Grandma Elena's new attorney had no way of knowing the truth behind these allegations.

Ralph's attorney's letter continued with what I considered a threat and a bit of advice.

If your office represents Joann Blum or had received compensation from Joann Blum, we hereby advise you that Ms. Blum's or her children's continued involvement in this matter without notice our office and Mr. Franklin is contrary to the Court's orders and jeopardizes Elena's safety. We will seek a temporary restraining order against Ms. Blum if she continues to engage in financial abuse and influencing Elena against Mr. Franklin.

Ralph's attorney knew Ralph had control of Grandma Elena's accounts, cash, and credit card. He assumed any retainer had been paid by me. Moreover, the attorney falsely stated as fact that I was engaged in financial abuse and influencing Grandma Elena against her son.

The letter continued.

Please contact our office as soon as possible so we can coordinate our efforts and ensure that Elena Franklin's safety is maintained. If you have information relating to Elena Franklin or Joann Blum we ask that you provide it immediately. We also will request that in the event you represent Joann Blum that you provide her a copy of this letter for her records and advise her of the legal consequences if she continues to interfere with Mr. Franklin's conservatorship.

There are legal processes that Ms. Blum can initiate and on which your office can assist that would present her case to the court if necessary.

I did not see this letter until after Grandma Elena's death. It explains why the attorney decided to refer Grandma Elena to a court appointed attorney.

When I sold liability insurance, I learned about trigger or buzz words. In insurance "negligence" is one of those words. As I read this letter I recognized the trigger words — financial abuse, undue influence, safety. Without proof or any offer of proof, those trigger words were used to make a point to the opposing attorney, one who had met with Grandma Elena for a mere 30 minutes.

Ralph's attorney charged Grandma Elena's estate in July 2012, for investigating "potential for assisted living for Elena vs. in-home assistance." Ralph insisted Grandma Elena's belief that he wanted to place her in assisted living proved the diagnosis of paranoid ideation.

I counter you are not paranoid if what you fear is actually happening. I had heard Ralph on multiple occasions say he thought Grandma Elena should be in a home. She was not making it up. He wanted to do it.

The Tide Turns

How much better would life be
if liars' pants actually caught on fire?
—Anonymous

After nine hours over four days of testing Grandma Elena, the psychologist reported.

Reason for Referral/Conclusions: Mrs. Franklin was referred for a psychological evaluation after she was deemed to be in need of a conservator by her primary care physician for financial matters. Based on a preponderance of evidence, some significant memory and learning decrements in aspects of verbal and visual information are clearly present. However, with reminder cues Mrs. Franklin functions commensurate to her peers in many aspects of her learning and memory abilities. In addition, some vital aspects of her mental status are still intact and in fact superior to a majority of her peers, and the current evaluation did not reveal paranoia, markedly impaired judgement, and/or poor reasoning ability warranting a conservatorship. Metrics involved in calculation, financial assessment and competency suggests that Mrs. Franklin demonstrates the ability to successfully identify financial obligations, demonstrates adequate insight and reasoning as it pertains to financial matters and has no evidence of financial difficulty based upon an examination of her credit report, and all financial documents provided to the evaluator.

It appears as though Mrs. Franklin does have memory decrements that will become progressively worse over time. However, at this time, there does not appear to be enough evidence that Mrs. Franklin possesses paranoia, poor judgement and/or the inability to accurately understand the nature and consequences of planning for her own financial future. It is clear that Mrs. Franklin will need some level of in-home care that should be decided in concert with Mrs. Franklin, her family, loved ones, mental health, medical and occupational therapeutic personnel. It is likely that Mrs. Franklin has a significant amount of discord with her personal relatives and may feel more secure with nonrelated individuals. At this time, Mrs. Franklin does appear to have some level of deficits that may eventually develop into incapacitation, however, at this time, there appears to be enough reality testing, logic, reasoning and overall financial proficiency to allow Mrs. Franklin to proceed with autonomous financial decision-making regarding her will/trust but it is equally likely that she will need some level of reminder cues and outside assistance in her home in order to handle day-to-day financial matters and activities of daily living (ADL).

Those results were encouraging. The doctor used the family and personal history information provided by Grandma Elena in his report. Also, important for the court was the information in another section.

Behavioral Observations. Mental Status Exam: Mrs. Franklin was seen over the course of four evaluation sessions. At all times, she was oriented toward person, place, time and the overall purpose of the assessment process. During times of extreme stress or when discussing situations regarding her anger as it pertains to her son pursuing conservatorship over her financial ability, Mrs. Franklin would occasionally have some level of frustration that somewhat interfered with the testing process. At no time did Mrs. Franklin appear to be delusional nor were there any themes indicative of someone that had psychotic processes. Mrs. Franklin genuinely believes that her son has malevolent intentions as it pertains to her being conserved and she believes that he will subsequently place her in an environment that she does not want to be placed into. He has in fact stated this to her...

I found it interesting that the report suggested by discussing Ralph and the conservatorship, Grandma Elena's ability to function was affected. Based on that report, I question why the court investigator did not make another visit to re-evaluate Grandma Elena.

Grandma Elena's court appointed attorney and his assistant insisted on driving her to and from the court hearings, even though we were available and had offered to provide transportation. I think those rides were the most expensive rides Grandma Elena ever took.

At the first hearing in July 2012, Ralph's role as temporary conservator was continued in spite of Grandma Elena's strenuous objections. Her court appointed attorney did not argue against the appointment. Outside the courtroom he told us, including Grandma Elena, that old people need to be taken care of by family just like small children. Her court appointed counsel was very well respected, and knowledgeable, but he came to court with predetermined assumptions, and conclusions. He concluded by saying that if she wasn't happy with his approach she could fire him and hire another attorney. He made it sound easy, but it was not that simple.

After that, Grandma Elena began writing letters to express herself to everyone involved. I checked with friends who had used estate attorneys, asking for recommendations. I contacted two attorneys and provided some general information about the case, but I didn't get a return call to set up a consultation from either. I did get an angry call from Ralph's attorney, who again threatened to have me prosecuted for contempt of court.

I had grown up with bullies in school and the neighborhood. The first time I confronted a bully, I was five years old. Since then, I have never backed down. While, I didn't know if that was a bluff, I felt I was on unfamiliar ground. Grandma Elena was already stressed and if the attorney was able to bring charge against me, she and my family would suffer. I would not only be risking myself, but my family could also be hurt and Grandma Elena would be thrown into even more turmoil. I didn't want to cause her any further anxiety, so I backed off.

That process made me realize I needed to set up my own estate. But I was afraid of stirring up trouble when I tried to hire an attorney to complete the task. In the end, I made an appointment with an attorney about 170 miles from my home. I hoped the distance would not trigger another unpleasant call from Ralph's attorney.

After Ralph took control of Grandma Elena's accounts, he stopped bringing groceries. Grandma Elena asked me to pick up some for her. I had been shopping for her for about a month, when I got the call from Ralph's attorney. The simple message — do not buy anything for Grandma Elena. You are interfering with Ralph's conservatorship and there will be consequences. If you think Grandma Elena needs something, contact Ralph and he will provide it if he agrees that it is something she needs.

I was instructed that no one other than Ralph had authorization to give Grandma Elena anything or perform any tasks for her. Ralph and the people Ralph instructed were the only ones allowed to help Grandma Elena. In the attorney's words, she needed to learn to depend on Ralph, and any deviation from this rule would result in legal consequences.

One of Grandma Elena's neighbors, someone I didn't know, called Adult Protective Services and reported Ralph for withholding financial support and food. Adult Protective Services notified the court investigator, but the investigation ended there.

In July 2012, Grandma Elena hand wrote a letter to the court investigator on a yellow legal-size tablet while sitting alone in her kitchen. Everything she wrote was correct, except the testing was 9 hours not 12. Grandma Elena did not receive a response. However,

Ralph did remove his personal property and the junk pile at the back fence.

Dear Linda

As of July 5, 2012, my son, Ralph Franklin was appointed my conservator by City Probate Court.

I do not want Ralph Franklin as my conservator because he has too many personal negative feelings toward me and makes them quite evident, especially by the tone of voice he uses when addressing me.

Ralph has, made too many financial problems to be allowed to control my assets and property.

Ralph and his wife and daughters have come to my home and been verbally abusive to me to the extent that I am physically afraid for them to be near me. On one occasion, I actually felt that I had been physically assaulted!!

Ralph has made no attempt to remove large amounts of his personal property stored in my house, my patio and my backyard. He has created a large junk pile against the fence in my backyard that attracts rats.

I want those things removed.

I also want to fire Tony Rodolfo as my court appointed attorney and be allowed to select another attorney, as Tony has made no attempt to represent me and has ignored my wishes.

I feel Tony Rodolfo has made a deal with my son and my son's attorney because he presented some statements in court that he did not discuss first with me.

I also ask you to have the court review the Jeffery Harrison Report. Dr. Harrison conducted twelve (12) hours of testing on me and does not recommend that I need a conservator!

If you call me regarding this situation, please tell me you are responding to this letter. Mornings preferable.

Sincerely
Elena L Franklin

The next morning, again while alone in her kitchen, Grandma Elena wrote a letter to her son using the same yellow legal tablet. I believe she didn't realize she'd stoked the flames by comparing things I did for her with things she felt Ralph should have done.

Ralph-

In your recent letter, you said we were working through our differences. How!!? Whenever I try to discuss anything with you, you get snarfy and walk out of the room!!

It's my gut feeling you are trying to gain control of my property and my assets — because I don't think you have any!!! And you don't want to face or discuss our issues! Just walking away won't solve anything and I am left sitting in an empty room! Abandoned!! Your behavior is snarfy and dismissive and you do not treat me with the respect due me!!

House Maintenance:

Where was your concern for my safety when Edward and Jo Ann had to put up a Life Alert Safety system that was needed for quite some time? Where was your concern about all the books on my floor (a tripping hazard) until Jo Ann removed them to book cases and shelves in the extra bedroom and the garage!!

Why are you now concerned about dangerous (your words) walkways on my property when they have been there for years? Is it because you want me to pay for getting them fixed before you take over my house???

Bank Account and Cash Availability

I have yet to see the debit card or any cash you left except for the wad of bills you threw on the buffet with obvious disdain.

Bills and Third-Party costs.

For at least my whole adult life, I have been able to maintain a comfortable lifestyle without any guidance from you! I particularly resent you think you should schedule my haircuts because I am proud of my "naturally curly hair."

People accessing my house and maintenance.

I resent your wanting to control the support staff for my house and garden who have worked for me for many years. They are just fine!!! Lopez is the son or cousin (I'm not sure) of the original Lopez who was hired by your father many years ago!!! It gives me great pleasure to talk with them when I pay them. They are interesting people and take great pride in their work! Cathy [housekeeper] is so afraid of you she goes over to Clara's house when you come by.

Please Back Off – Let me have my own life. I don't want any of your family near me since they clearly don't like or respect me – even your presence in my home makes me afraid.

In the interest of my safety and the appearance of my property, I ask you to remove the boxes of your and your family's belongings from my patio and yard and any other place you have stacked them. And please remove the trash pile you created by the fence. Please do this at your expense – not mine.

Remember!! I'm a survivor!

Mom

Copies went to Grandma Elena's attorney, the court investigator, and an attorney in the office with Ralph's attorney.

In August 2012, Grandma Elena wrote to her attorney. This time she used school binder paper while sitting alone in her kitchen.

Tony-

I ask you to resign as my court appointed lawyer so I can hire a lawyer who will fight for my rights. You have shown no indication of doing so to date.

It is my wish to fight this plan to conserve me! I do not believe I need to be conserved. As proof of this I have attached Dr. Jeffery Harrison's report.

Please note in the report that Dr. Smith [Grandma Elena's family physician] agreed to support Dr. Harrison's findings.

Tony – you totally ignored my demand that my son, Ralph, not be appointed as my conservator. Ralph has too many issues regarding our personal relationship to be allowed to have this power!!! He has his own personal agenda that does not include having my well-being at heart! – only his own!! Ralph lies!

A good example of this is his claim that I do not shower! I am insulted!! To set the record straight, I shower on alternate days due to having extra dry skin! My hair is shampooed daily. I am amused at his sudden interest in my personal hygiene.

Dr. Harrison did indicate that I have short term memory loss. I manage this very well in my normal routine. If you have noticed this condition in me it is more pronounced when I am under stress or tired. Lawyers should not interview their 90 year old clients at 5 o'clock in the afternoon!!

At this time, I am well supported by many of my neighbors and friends and by my (unofficial) adopted family who can't believe lies he has told about me. They always thought he was a fine fellow! These people spend more time with me than Ralph and his family ever have and know me much better.

I wish to be surrounded by people who love and respect me – not by people like Ralph & his family who make a point of coming into my home and tell me I am a terrible person and they have hated me for years and wish to sever all ties with me – as Ralph and his wife and daughters have done. Ralph comes by when he wants money!

By filing those papers against me Ralph interrupted my process of hiring additional personal home assistance and delayed my receiving their help.

Please comply with my request for you to resign and thus allow me to hire someone to represent my interests as I see them

Sincerely
Elena Franklin

Grandma Elena sent a copy of this letter to the court investigator.

Grandma Elena's attorney and the court investigator finally did visit her. They wanted to know "who had been with her" when she wrote out a holographic will. No one had been with her. She had written it while alone in her kitchen. She wrote it on a yellow note pad. Grandma Elena admitted she had written it, but stated she didn't remember under what conditions. She also asked if she could leave her estate to the Masonic Home for Retirees.

Grandma Elena was convinced she was being punished for wanting to disinherit her son. She believed everyone working on her case was on Ralph's side. In fact, she was willing to give the estate to Ralph if he would let her live out the rest of her life in peace, but it was too late for appeasement.

The letters she wrote appeared to have no impact on the court's decision.

Ralph in Charge

Losing your life is not the worst thing that can happen.
The worst thing is to lose your reason for living.
—Jo Nesbø

In July 2012, Ralph came by Grandma Elena's house while I was there. He summarized the events.

Purchased items at Costco for Mom. Tried to deliver them. JoAnn was there. Mom would not accept items (left them there anyway). Said she did not need any food — but said ice box was empty — I said no — I just brought you food other day. Asked if she had a grocery list — replied no — don't need anything from you! Asked JoAnn if there was a list over there. She shook her head "no," after glancing over there. (Mom habitually writes things down so I suspect there may have been a list but will not dispute).

Mom started getting ugly — saying Dad would be ashamed of me for treating her like this. I said he would be proud of me for stepping in and taking care of you! "No, he wouldn't!!! You don't know your own father. I never want you in my house again!"

All Ralph brought that day was a 24-can case of Pepsi and a large container of peanuts. There was no list by the refrigerator. When Ralph asked about the mail, I tried to hand him the junk mail, but Grandma Elena snatched it away. I thought she was going to hit Ralph with it. She continued screaming at him to get out.

When Ralph's attorney called me the next day, he referred to the events when Ralph attempted to deliver groceries. He was very angry with me, saying I should have stepped in and helped mother and son resolve the situation. After all the calls telling me to stay out of Ralph's relationship with his mother, I was amazed he was calling to yell at me for not stepping in.

While my visits did not include any discussion of money, estate, Ralph or his family, over the summer of 2012, I did let Grandma Elena vent. I thought she needed a place to unload her negative feelings. After a while, though, Grandma Elena began repeating the same negative stories — some from long ago. I sat down with her and told her I was happy to listen. However, I really wanted our visits to be like they always had been, about us, about what the kids were doing, my current projects, and, of course, we would continue to solve the world's problems.

We had so much to talk about and I often had pictures and videos to share. Activities my grandkids were involved in often brought back memories of their mothers' childhoods. I reminded Grandma Elena that someday I would not be able to sit at her kitchen table and I wanted to have happy memories to try to fill the void.

In hindsight, I realize I had made an enormous mistake. I continued to believe the struggle going on between Grandma Elena and Ralph was between them. Once Ralph and his attorney used my friendship as a weapon, I was pulled into the battle. If I had had the foresight to hire my own attorney, I think things would have been different. I thought I was protecting Grandma Elena from further turmoil. In fact, by not stating the truth about my involvement, I was letting Ralph and his attorneys define the narrative of events.

I was at Grandma Elena's later that summer when a neighbor stopped by. A few minutes later her husband stopped by to say he was going out and had locked their front door. He wanted to be sure she had a key. Ralph claimed I was bringing strange men to Grandma Elena's house. People in the neighborhood that Ralph didn't know had a history of stopping in to visit Grandma Elena.

The next day, I got a call from the court investigator yelling at me. She said, "You are not to bring strange men to Grandma Elena's house. I want to know who you brought there."

In August, Ralph wrote a letter to me, my husband, both of my daughters, and their husbands, as well as my son.

As you are all aware, I have been appointed conservator over my mother, Elena Franklin's person and estate. My obligations as conservator require me to manage and supervise her affairs to ensure her safety and protection.

I know that everyone is concerned about her and wishes to make all aspects of her life as pleasurable and enjoyable as possible. And I hope that you will continue in this effort and allow me to assist in this endeavor. I thank each of you for supporting Elena and me during this process and encourage your friendship and companionship with her in the future.

I have retained the services of a part-time certified caregiver to assist my mom during this period. I have asked her to inform me of my mom's needs. I would appreciate it if we could arrange for a time for all of you to meet Rita prior to you visiting during times she is present. This will facilitate your continued visits with my mom. Rita has helped other individuals who have given us stellar reviews of her services. We are very fortunate to have her assisting us in this matter. Rita is in high demand and we were very lucky that she was available to help us.

Rita will primarily, with my assistance and oversight, take care of many of the daily tasks for Mom including: grocery shopping; taking Mom shopping or to the movies; encouraging Mom to take morning and afternoon walks; possibly participating in *Avenitas* or other social events; helping with laundry; making snacks or breakfast or lunch for her; possibly helping with other cooking or meals; providing companionship; and performing other tasks as needed.

Rita's activities and responsibilities will in no way diminish the continued support by Cathy.

While we appreciate the contributions all of you, as well as other friends and neighbors such as Clara, have made in the past towards helping my mom, Rita or I will be able to take care of those tasks from now on, leaving you to enjoy your visits with Mom free from any chores or tasks. I hope that this will allow you to focus on Mom during your visits since I know that my mom enjoys your company.

I, with the assistance of lawyers and court staff, have decided to ensure my mom's safety at the house by installing CO_2 monitors, smoke detectors, transferring the medical alert to my attention, repurposing house keys, informing all parties of my role and responsibilities in caring for Mom, and making certain repairs to the house as needed.

My primary concern has been my mom's lack of understanding of her financial situation. My role is to undertake a complete evaluation and assist in preserving her estate so that she is able to live comfortably. I have received copies of Elena's bank statements from past years and I will be reviewing them to ensure that all accounts are in order. I understand the accounts have not been managed in recent years and that certain transactions that she has completed are questionable.

Please do not assist my mother in any financial or estate planning. I have received a copy of certain documents that my mother attempted to modify and I will retain them in my possession. As you were informed at the hearing, all powers of attorney of any kind have been revoked. No one has the authority to engage in any financial transaction of any kind with my mom without my authorization.

As I have expressed before, I am concerned with my mother's "paranoid ideation" as described by Dr. Smith. Be assured that there is no intention of removing mom from her home. She will remain there as long as possible. Because of these paranoid thoughts of my mother, it is of utmost importance that she is not asked to make payments, gifts, or any other financial contributions to any person or organization without my authorization and that she is not asked to modify, write, or prepare any estate document transferring, modifying, or otherwise any estate plan without my notification. I will notify the court of any suspicious activities taken by my mother in relation to these matters and have been advised that I have a legal right to seek review of any transaction or pursue any parties in violation of the Court's orders.

All other service providers have been informed of my role and I have coordinated visits and maintenance plans with them.

I encourage all of you to maintain your friendship and companionship with mom. Due to her volatility and susceptibility to undue influence, any statement action or comment that is negative or relating to my role or any other person's will cause financial and physical harm. I hope that you understand that mom may hurt herself or others if certain information is discussed. She is 90 years old and I hope that you understand that she should be living her life without any of these stresses. I will appreciate and require if you visit mom that you are prohibited and refrain from discussing the following topics:

- Any issues any of you have with my family. I am her son and love her and will always care for and protect her.

- She does not need to engage in any discussion relating to her estate. Roy Metcalf has been advised of the letters of conservatorship and as you heard at the hearing, Mr. Rodolfo agreed that Mom is susceptible to undue influence;

- Health planning, medical appointments, change of physicians, re-evaluations, dental appointments, and related medical affairs.

If you feel there is a situation that needs attention, please bring it directly to my attention. If you are unable to reach me, please advise Rita or Clara and they will get in contact with me to make the appropriate arrangements. Clara is right across the street from Mom so should there ever be any sort of emergency where I cannot be contacted, please contact her about the situation. She has agreed to assist in such circumstances. I have provided her contact information below.

If you wish take mom to lunch, dinner, movie or any event you are welcome to do so provided I am contacted prior to such an event and it is commensurate with her condition at the time.

Under no circumstances is my mom to be transported long distances, over mountains, or where changes in altitude may affect her vertigo.

If clarification of any of the foregoing is needed, please call as I am willing to discuss these matters to the extent that court direction allows.

My contact information is below. Please use it to reach me for any situation involving my mother.

Ralph

I didn't need clarification. Ralph's attorney had already called to state he would prevent me from visiting Grandma Elena if I tried to do anything for her. This included buying things she asked for, changing a light bulb, or other little tasks around the house, including picking up trip hazards. I was not allowed to bring gifts, but I did send flowers on special occasions. I was up against the limits of the rules as spelled out by Ralph and his counsel.

One afternoon in early August, I walked into Grandma Elena's living room and saw she had cut three lovely roses from her garden, and placed them in a vase across from her chair.

"I see you've cut some pretty roses from your garden."

"Yes, I needed some beauty in my life with all this ugliness."

Grandma Elena was a survivor, creating a corner of beauty in a terrible crisis.

Invitation to the Spider's Parlor

"Will you walk into my parlor?"
said the spider to the fly.
—Mary Howitt

In August, I received a request to attend a meeting with Ralph and his attorney at the attorney's office. The common consensus of my family and friends was don't go. Everyone felt I was walking into a trap. Still, I hoped I could mediate the situation in some way. I was naive and foolish to believe I would be heard. I now know I should never have attended the meeting without my own attorney.

During the first half hour, Ralph's attorney lectured me on the difference between growing up in a household and simply being a neighbor who lives down the street and had occasional contact with her.

True, I had not been raised by Grandma Elena and yet, I would never describe my relationship with Grandma Elena as one of occasional contact. We were far more than neighbors living down the street from each other and Ralph knew it.

I believe the description given by Supreme Court Justice Sonia Sotomayor of close friends who became family to her in My Beloved World, applied to us. Her description reassured me that the way Elena and Frank became my children's grandparents did not sound strange.

Over 40 years, a deep enduring bond of love and caring had grown between my family and Grandma Elena and Papa Frank, who had described our relationship as "love relatives."

My youngest daughter, Megan, was in second grade when an aide at school asked her, "Who from your family is coming to Back to School Night?"

Megan replied, "My Mom and Dad and Charlotte and Ethan and Grandma Elena."

The aide said, "Grandma Elena? She's like a real grandmother?"

Megan proclaimed, "She is my real grandmother."

Still confused by the comment made by the school aide, Megan went to Grandma Elena's house after school and repeated the conversation.

"Why did she say that you are not real?"

Grandma Elena's reply was sweet and profound. "She didn't know that we are family by love."

"What is that?"

"We are related because we love each other, the strongest bond of all."

During the conservatorship hearings, Ralph and his attorney chose to describe me as "friend/former neighbor and financial predator." Ralph seemed to have changed his views from the past. When Papa Frank died, the obituary written by Grandma Elena and Ralph listed my children as "also survived by."

So, the question becomes, who has the right to define you and your relationship? No one from the court asked Grandma Elena or me to define our relationship.

My children had grown up referring to Ralph and his wife, Doris, as uncle and aunt. In the past we had a very close relationship. That's why they became Ethan's Godparents. Beginning in the Middle Ages the role of Godparents was to serve as a second set of parents. Godparents today standup in church and make serious commitments to their Godchild. My family believes the Godparent/Godchild relationship should not be taken lightly.

So, what makes family? Is it just an accident of birth or marriage? Does love count? Should it count? Should the court take into consideration the length and intensity of the relationship when considering who should be considered family?

After the lawyer finished, he asked if there were things I thought Ralph could do to improve the situation. I explained how important it was to Grandma Elena to be able to pay her housekeeper and gardener herself. It gave her pleasure to make the simple gesture. It made her feel she had control of her environment. I felt it would be an open hand offer from Ralph signaling he was willing to work with Grandma Elena. My suggestions fell on deaf ears.

Ralph still wasn't finished making restrictions on Grandma Elena. In the middle of August, he wrote this letter.

Joann:

Thank you again very much for meeting with me last week and providing me with your observations. I very much appreciate your input. As you know, I have been appointed the conservator for my mother's estate and person, and as I mentioned, I am legally required to as the conservator to ensure my mother's health and safety. I would like to inform you and your family that I appreciate your help with my mother and I know that she and you have been friends for some time. The court determined that my mother is and continues to be very susceptible to undue influence by others and it is my responsibility to ensure that she is protected against any possible influences that may affect her thinking or her person.

As such, it is important that I monitor her visits and outings very carefully. Her vertigo and other health conditions do not allow her to travel on long trips and her immediate recollection is severely impaired. I have discussed measures with my attorney and the court's investigators to ensure that compliance with the law and protection of my mother are met. The following procedures are required to ensure my compliance with the law and, more importantly, the safety and protection of my mother. As I mentioned in our meeting, I would like to ask that you and your family, and any other person with whom you are familiar in this matter to be informed of these procedures to ensure my mother's safety.

Due to the severity of my mother's condition, it will be of utmost importance that everyone comply with these measures. I am always open to suggestions or other recommendations, such as those that you mentioned, and that I will be applying in the future. Any diversion from these procedures may result in harm to my mother, and my pursuit of any claims against persons taking actions in contravention of these procedures. Any interaction with Mom has the potential to lead to her mental or physical harm should something inappropriate happen and I want to ensure that we minimize this in the future.

- Any person intending to visit Elena must notify me in writing (email is acceptable) of their visit. I understand that you periodically visit with mother for 1 hour during your lunch hour. If you will continue to do this, I will calendar this visit weekly. Please notify me on the days you will stay longer or will not attend the visit. Please provide me with a list of the persons that you consider will visit my mother, including your children, grandchildren, spouses or any other person related or unrelated to you. I need to ensure that all persons visiting my mother are not strangers and will not be present alone with my mother at any one time.

- Long trips (more than 1/2 hour) are restricted unless I have been notified in writing no less than two (2) days prior to the trip and her health condition is discussed with her principal physician. Your family should provide the same notifications if they intend to take her on a trip, although I would recommend that we not engage in trips until her situation is more stable. If notifications are not made, it will impact my decisions about who spends time with my mother. I need to know who she is with, where, and for how long in order to protect her from undue influence and keep her safe from harm.

- I have informed everyone visiting my mother that work will be done to the house for my mother's safety. This includes work on the sidewalk surrounding the property and the installation of a handrail for the right side of the patio door. I will be working with Mom to determine what times are most convenient for her for these repairs. Please be aware that if you stop by, this work may be in progress and safety precautions should be taken.

- A Life Alert system has been installed and programmed with the appropriate emergency numbers. If an emergency should occur while you are with my mother and you cannot get in touch with me using the contact information I have provided, use the Life Alert system.

- I have delivered a tape recorder so that Mom can tape messages and conversations that I can deliver to Gene. This may be an activity she would enjoy working on with you during your visits since she talks to you about Gene.

- I have arranged for Gene to visit from August 31st to September 4th. He will be staying with mom and I will be there nights as well. If you or your family intends to visit during these days, please notify me. I would like to ensure that my mother and Gene both feel comfortable with your visits.

- As I mentioned to you, food is provided to my mother on a weekly basis, however, if she mentions any item for which she forgets to tell me but tells you, please write a list and leave it next to the refrigerator for me. Since you will be having lunch with her, I want to make sure that your visits are focused on her remembering her past and enjoying your company and not on the chores.

- Caretakers have been arranged to visit mother and care for her needs. My mother will have days calendared to visit doctors, hairdressers and other personal matters during the week which the caretakers and myself will arrange.

- "Papa" (a neighbor) – Clara's father - will be moving the trash, recycle, and yard waste bins to the street on early Thursday mornings and retrieving them on Thursday evenings. This is a job for him and allows him to feel wanted and needed. I will be using him for other tasks as well when they arise. Mom is familiar and comfortable with him.

In my previous correspondence I identified other neighbors and parties that will be assisting my mother and I hope that with you and your family's help we can make my mother's living more enjoyable.

I have notified others of these procedures and expect everyone to comply with them accordingly.

As I mentioned to you, it is imperative that we all work together to make my mother's situation better and I hope that all of this work and procedures will make my mother's situation better.

Shortly I will be posting a weekly schedule of mom's weekly & monthly activities including doctor appointments, haircuts, and other activities. As Rita's schedule is developed, and as various changes to the schedule are made, I will provide the schedule to you. In the event you wish to visit on a specific date or take mom on an outing, please contact me directly and I will add it to the schedule if there is no conflict. In addition, there is attached to this letter, a listing of folks that you may wish to have access or visitations to mom. Please provide the requested contact information so that I may provide them with schedules as well, and return it to me. I will provide this access list to the caregivers as well.

Until I produce and publish mom's schedule, please limit your visitations to occasional short duration lunch time periods.

Thank you again,
Ralph

The court did not rule consistent with his claims. The judge also did not say that Ralph should control her thinking or her person.

Grandma Elena's court appointed attorney responded to Ralph's attorney.

Ralph's two letters to Jo Ann Blum were inappropriate to say the least. Whether as temporary conservator or as permanent conservator, Ralph is not empowered to control who visits Elena, when they visit Elena, and for how long they visit Elena. Nor must those persons who wish to visit Elena notify her conservator in advance before doing so.

The court investigator informed Ralph in an e-mail:

Ralph, the rules have got to go (per Tony as well) as they're too heavy-handed.

Nothing more was ever done to remove the visitation restrictions.

In order to keep peace, I shared this letter with the friends and neighbors I knew visited Grandma Elena. One of them felt that Grandma Elena should know what Ralph was requiring concerning visits and showed her the letter. Grandma Elena became upset and called the court investigator, which resulted in a nasty call from Ralph's attorney.

I responded via e-mail to Ralph's attorney.

In response to your call yesterday, here is the clarification.

The letter that was originally attached to this e-mail paragraph 2 last sentence said.

"As I mentioned in our meeting, I would like to ask that you and your family, and any other person with whom you are familiar in this matter be informed of these procedures to ensure my mother's safety."

This is why I sent the e-mail to the persons with whom I am familiar in the matter. My family was already included in the original e-mail.

Ralph further emphasizes his insistence on this being done in paragraph 3, third sentence:

"Any diversion from these procedures may result in harm to my mother, and my pursuit of any claims against persons taking actions in contravention of these procedures."

A Prisoner in Her Own Home

Friends don't spy; true friendship is about privacy, too.
—Stephen King, *Hearts in Atlantis*

Grandma Elena told me that no repairs were being made to the house, although there were things that needed to be done for her safety. Ralph didn't follow through on any of my suggestions. There were no trips or lunches out, no outings of any kind any more.

After Ralph's edict, Grandma Elena became a prisoner in her own home with Clara watching from across the street to ensure she didn't go out. Nor could Grandma Elena have called for help because no strangers were allowed in the house. No schedule was ever published. Worst of all, Grandma Elena was not included in the selection of Rita for caregiver/companion, leaving her to believe that Rita was there to spy on her and report back to Ralph.

I was shocked he made an arrangement at the end of August for Gene to come to visit and be cared for by Grandma Elena. Ralph described Grandma Elena's health as severe, arguing that her deteriorating health was the reason for not allowing her to go out. And yet, he let his mother be responsible for Gene for five days. Ralph only stayed a couple of the nights during Gene's visit. I don't mean to imply Gene should not have visited. I believe Grandma Elena would have benefited from substantial help from a caregiver for Gene during his stay.

Grandma Elena was back in court for the next conservatorship hearing in September 2012. I had been warned by Ralph's attorney not to get involved. In fact, he implied he would take legal action against me if I showed up. While I did not want to inflame the situation any more than it already was, I couldn't let Grandma Elena go to court alone. When I explained the situation to a couple of friends, they agreed to go in my place.

I was told Grandma Elena's attorney asked if anyone would like to address the court. That was a great piece of showmanship on his part. He had not advised anyone he would be asking for testimonials, so no one had a chance to prepare.

I was told Grandma Elena was coherent when she stood and spoke in court about not wanting to be conserved. She stated that if the court thought she had to be conserved she did not want Ralph. She also requested the judge appoint a different attorney.

The judge ignored her since everyone, except the psychologist, claimed she was being subjected to some terrible "undue influence," including her attorney. The judge ordered another psychological review, he then announced he would rule after reading the second report.

He wanted a second independent opinion, but that is not what he got.

In October, just before Grandma Elena was scheduled for the new battery of tests, she broke a molar in the back of her mouth. Ralph was the only one allowed to take her to the dentist.

Ralph instructed the dentist to pull the tooth, and also indicated he would not authorize any additional work such as replacing the tooth. Grandma Elena became upset. She was proud she had all her teeth, and she resented Ralph for making the decision without consulting her. Pulling the tooth was the quickest and cheapest solution.

Later that afternoon, a neighbor stopped in to visit. She knew nothing about the broken tooth or the trip to the dentist. She found Grandma Elena alone, in pain, bleeding and very upset. Grandma Elena asked her to call me for help. I told the neighbor I didn't have the care instructions, so she would have to call Ralph. She was reluctant, since she had already had one bad experience with him. She called and he brought the care instructions to the house.

The neighbor called to tell me how shocked she was at how rude, officious and disrespectful Ralph had been to Grandma Elena just for interrupting his day a second time. I told her there was nothing I could do to help. I was an identified enemy and Ralph was her temporary conservator.

Later that day, I went by to check on Grandma Elena. She was still upset with Ralph's actions at the dentist and the loss of her tooth. She complained there would be a hole, which would interfere with chewing. I suggested she try chewing on the other side of her mouth. I hoped once it healed and she got used to the missing tooth she'd relax. After that, she calmed down. She did become accustomed to the missing tooth and accepted it, but never forgave Ralph for the way he treated her.

Grandma Elena's attorney and the court investigator worked with Ralph and his attorney to arrange for the second evaluation.

Ralph, and the caregiver Ralph had hired, drove Grandma Elena to the appointment in mid-October 2012. They waited in the outer office while she was tested and then drove her home. That testing session lasted nine hours with no break for lunch or a trip to the lady's room.

I remember taking the tests to obtain my insurance license, two tests of four hours each. So, I signed up to take both on the same day. When colleagues heard I was attempting both tests on the same day, they argued I was crazy. At the time, I was half Grandma Elena's age and there was a two-hour lunch break. The tests were multiple choice answers, which allowed me to go at my own pace. I completed the tests early, in effect only testing for six hours. Afterward, I was so drained I found it hard to drive home. I couldn't imagine nine hours of non-stop tests as well as the stress of knowing what was on the line.

As part of the report, the psychologist included background on the Franklin family as well as my family. The information about my family was provided to the examiner by Ralph's attorney, not a neutral source. No one called me to ask for information. When I saw the final report, I was appalled at the inaccuracy of the information provided about the five of us.

Ralph was asked to complete a Neuropsychiatric profile as well as provide background information, financial records, and report on observations made by Grandma Elena's neighbor, Clara.

I wonder how different things would have looked to the examiner if Ralph had produced a copy of Grandma Elena's credit report that showed she had never been 30 days late with a payment. But, that credit report was only provided to the first examiner.

I believe the information provided and the manner the second psychological examination was handled helped skew the results for conservatorship. I knew why Ralph cared. He was about to be disinherited and he needed to stop the process. It would not matter to Ralph if Grandma Elena gave her estate to my family or to charity. The end result would be the same. He would not have the money.

What I didn't understand was why Ralph's attorney pushed for conservatorship, until I saw the orders for payment. Ralph was being allowed to pay his attorney's fees with Grandma Elena's savings. Ralph had made it clear during the meeting at his house that he had no money to pay for Grandma Elena's care. I'm sure that fact was not lost on Ralph's attorney. If they lost, how would he get paid? In the end, Grandma Elena paid for both of the psychological evaluations, the court investigator, Ralph's attorney, and her court appointed attorney, the one she tried to fire. Ralph's conservatorship battle proved to be a financial and emotional cost for Grandma Elena.

Before the court battle, Grandma Elena often expressed appreciation about the kind neighbors who were willing to look out for her. She talked about Clara checking that she had brought in her morning paper. If Grandma Elena got up late and didn't get the paper, Clara would check on her. Grandma Elena appreciated knowing someone noticed any change in her routine. She recalled a time several years earlier when Clara almost lost her house after she became a widow. Grandma Elena paid the past due mortgage payments. In Grandma Elena's mind, they were two widows trying to make it in the world. When Grandma Elena became aware that Clara now reported her movements to Ralph, she felt spied on, and betrayed.

In an attempt to make her feelings clear, Grandma Elena wrote two letters to the psychologist. He attached an excerpt from each to the end of his report.

1. Ms. Franklin' October 17, 2012, 9:15pm

    JoAnn came by to see me and I told her that I had felt I had been treated fairly by you and that I had been told you thought I had cleared up any misunderstandings of our relationship – that she had no ulterior motives toward me – but just a very dear friend of many years – we have many common interests – books – sewing – crafts – and her two wonderful girls. Again, I digress...

    I'm not stupid – I realize that there are people who do not wish me well – mostly – unfortunately – mostly Ralph – This is the greatest failure of my life and I failed to recognize warning signs.

    I want to stay in my own home (I certainly have earned that), pick my own friends and not be treated like a strange person to be studied and spied on and discussed and written about by learned medical experts. I now feel like I'm living in a fish bowl!

    I feel so exposed – every move – every thought – scrutinized and studied and interpreted by the experts. And why is this so??? Because Ralph wants to control me and all I own – whether it be my friends – my possessions or my soul.

    I AM TIRED OF BEING A MEDICAL PROJECT!

2. 3:41am (6 hours after the first) on October 18, 2012

    I'm tired – and I know this situation will go on and on – but I want you to know Ralph should never be allowed to handle my financial affairs – and especially control who can be my friends.

I want you to know I don't want Ralph to be my conservator – he's a control freak and I know he won't stop trying to get complete legal power over me and my life!

New Not So Normal

The ache for home lives in all of us.
The safe place where we can go as we are
and not be questioned.
—Maya Angelou, *All God's Children*

In October 2012, I went for my usual noon visit with Grandma Elena. To my surprise, my husband stopped on his way to meet with a client. He had a book on the Boer War that he wanted to loan Grandma Elena. The book was a follow up to an earlier conversation. He also brought a couple of military history magazines he wanted to give her.

They talked for a bit about military history and the Boer War, in particular, and then he left for his meeting. I left soon after. Grandma Elena expressed her appreciation for the book and magazines. She was looking forward to spending the afternoon reading them.

Early the next morning, I received a call from the Court Investigator demanding to know the identity of the man I had brought to Grandma Elena's house. She stressed that it was unsafe to bring men to Grandma Elena's house. My scheduled visits were to be just me. She had received a report of my husband's unannounced visit.

Grandma Elena told me, "Clara now spies on me and reports to Ralph about everything that happens here."

I assured the court investigator my husband had stopped in to bring Grandma Elena a book and magazines.

As a consequence, that was my husband's last visit. He had grown up in another country and having his comings and goings reported to the court was just too creepy for him. I wondered how many others felt the same way and had stopped visiting Grandma Elena.

Ralph and his attorney continued to demand restricted visits. We were told again and again not to take Grandma Elena out without Ralph's permission. In the end, Grandma Elena had no more lunches or dinner outings, no movies or trips to the bookstore.

On October 24, Ralph received the second draft of the psychiatric report to check for factual errors. Too bad Grandma Elena or I weren't asked to review it. We could have pointed out many errors. In the report, the examiner recounted the bizarre battle over Sandra's ice skates.

That same morning, Grandma Elena found Sandra's second place skating medal on her kitchen counter. She called me very upset that someone had come into her house while she slept. She had complained for weeks about Ralph doing the same thing, in an effort to confuse and fluster her. I had discounted her suspicions until this incident. I was afraid if she complained to the court without evidence, it would have a negative reflection on her.

That time I suggested she call the court investigator and explain what happened. The court investigator, in turn, reported to Ralph.

Morning!

Got a call from your mother this morning. She awoke this morning to find a silver ice skating award medal – inscribed with East Ridge Ice Arena 14th District Championship – on her kitchen counter. She's a little freaked out. Said Sandra is an ice skater and she's "creeped" out at the thought of someone entering her home during the night. I asked if there was any possibility that the medal is from years ago and it just happened to land on her counter during cleaning. She didn't recall. Elena asked if she should say something to you or just ignore it. I told her to do whatever made her more comfortable. She said she'll just ignore it ☺ Just thought you'd want to know.

Hope all is well.

Ralph replied by e-mail.

WOW!

It was Sandra's from around 1989...

Cathy or Rita probably found it cleaning Tuesday evening and put it out for her!

With the front door chained, the back door and sliding glass door dead-bolted, and mom being a very light sleeper...I can't come up with how someone might have got in any why!

Funny though...Rita called last night (Wednesday) and told me mom is back on the rampage about selling her house and giving the money to who she wants and nobody can do anything about it.

I was over Tuesday after work and she was having difficulty understanding the calendar and her appointments...several have changed and were marked on the calendar for her. She called the house several times Wednesday morning wanting to know if she should bring the handicap parking tag with her for the appointment. I didn't get the message until late Wednesday night as I was in Yountville talking to Gene's doctors and then to work in Walnut Creek for the rest of the day.

Dr. Glass previously told me that she is experiencing difficulty in combining visual information and processing it with memory and consequences/results.

In addition, both Monday and Tuesday, she called me a number of times each day to ask where her garage door opener was — she misplaced it several weeks ago and it had not turned up yet. (This happened a couple of months ago, and then it finally turned up in an odd place after about 2 weeks).

There are a few problems with Ralph's version of events. First, he had taken the chain off the front door early in October 2012, 14 days before this incident. Cathy or Rita were never at Grandma Elena's after she went to bed for the night. The investigator could have called and asked them if they found the medal, but again no follow up call was made. I had gone inside many times when Grandma Elena was napping and she hadn't awoken. In addition, Ralph often stopped by early in the morning and left a note for Grandma Elena on her mailbox, so she'd know he was going when he went to see Gene. The remainder of his email had nothing to do with the skating medal. I think he wanted to build his case for her "deterioration."

If someone I didn't trust snuck into my home while I was asleep, I would have been creeped out as well. I couldn't blame Grandma Elena for getting upset.

Ralph Has Absolute Power

Stand up for yourself.
Never give any one
permission to abuse you.
—Lailah Gifty Akita

In November 2012, the judge appointed Ralph permanent conservator. This was no surprise considering the second psychological report recommended Grandma Elena be conserved.

When her case was called, Grandma Elena walked up to the defense table to stand by her lawyer. She was determined to once again plead not to be conserved. Her court appointed attorney still disagreed with her and didn't mount a defense. She spoke again, asking to be allowed to live the rest of her life in peace. Even given her pleas and the reports of experts, including the court investigator, the judge ruled, "I'm going to do something you are not going to like." He then appointed her son Ralph as conservator.

As the words hung in the air, I could see Grandma Elena's posture change. From where I sat, she looked like someone recovering from a punch. I looked over at Doris and Cynthia seated across the room from me. They were smiling. They had won. Their future was secure. Grandma Elena would not be allowed to disinherit Ralph.

Ralph's attorney then asked to vacate the new Power of Attorney, and Durable Power of Attorney for Health Care, that Grandma Elena signed to take those powers from Ralph. The judge agreed, and it was over. Ralph had all the power.

Grandma Elena turned and began to walk out of the court room. I joined her and we walked together. As we went through the doors into the hall, she looked at me and asked. "What just happened?"

"Ralph is your conservator." I drew a deep breath, put my arm around her shoulder and added. "It's going to be alright. We can make it work." I had no idea how since I was in uncharted water. I wanted to give her the hope she had given to me so many times in the past.

In a letter to the court investigator, Grandma Elena had stated her preferences, describing my family as her "unofficial adopted family." Unofficial became the operative word. In the end, it left us with "no standing" in the court's eyes. It meant we could not advocate for her. We had no right to see her in her final days and hours.

Grandma Elena wrote she didn't want to be surrounded by people who didn't wish her well, people like Ralph and his family. Rather, she wanted to be surrounded by people who loved her, my family.

The court proceedings left questions, and red flags, mistakes made out of ignorance, good intentions, and fear. As I was writing this book, I began to understand a great deal more about conservatorships, estate planning, and probate court. I know now how Grandma Elena could have protected herself from Ralph.

Adults who find it difficult or impossible to handle their affairs can benefit from conservatorship. I believe, in the case of Grandma Elena, conservatorship was used to subdue the will of a 90-year-old woman and take away her ability to control her life and estate. By becoming Grandma Elena's conservator, Ralph was guaranteed he would not be disinherited. He was also given control of how much money was spent on Grandma Elena's care. He no longer had to worry about being kind, respectful or courteous. He would no longer be held accountable for his behavior in his emotional and daily interactions with his mother.

We were unprepared for what happened to Grandma Elena in her final days. One of the greatest regrets of my life was not being able to protect Grandma Elena or help her retain control of her lifestyle.

Ralph was ordered to provide Grandma Elena a debit card with a $100 balance, which she didn't know how to use. The permanent order meant that for the rest of her days, Ralph would continue to require Grandma Elena to ask him for money every time she wanted to buy something.

I reminded Grandma Elena there could be no positive result in battling with Ralph. He held the power and he made it clear every chance he got. When she'd ask him why he was doing something, his reply was simple, "Because I can."

Grandma Elena was determined to continue the fight. She did have the right of appeal. However her court appointed attorney had been released at the last hearing, so she had no attorney and no information on what rights she had left.

We only knew what Ralph and his attorney told us. We kept hearing Grandma Elena no longer had rights. We later found out that was false.

One day, I came in and found Grandma Elena had replaced Zander's picture with the painting her neighbor had made especially for her. Even though I suggested the change was a bad idea, her defiant response was, Ralph could not dictate what she looked at in her own home. Grandma Elena added she had not seen Zander for years and believed she would not recognize him if he crossed her path.

Ralph and his family stopped inviting Grandma Elena to holiday meals or family celebrations years before. Ralph would take a plate of food to Grandma Elena at her house, after the family finished their celebration. Grandma Elena was hurt by this. She would grab the plate and throw it in the trash, turkey, mash potatoes and all. She happily accepted food when neighbors brought her meals or baked goods. She'd make them a cup of tea, and enjoy their company while she ate.

Grandma Elena knew she could no longer order Ralph out of her house or stop him from taking things, so she got revenge by pretending not to remember. She knew it annoyed him so she used it as a weapon. I cautioned her, several times, not to do it, but she couldn't resist torturing him.

Over the next few months, we settled into an uneasy but calm state. I stopped getting angry calls from Ralph's attorney. During visits, Grandma Elena and I were able to focus on the things we liked best. We went back to solving the world's problems and, for the most part, ignored Ralph.

I had never spoken against Ralph and his family. Grandma Elena's anger was driven by their mistreatment. Their actions and words were what made her dislike them so much.

In February 2013, Grandma Elena called to say that Ralph was afraid her life was in danger. I asked her to tell me the whole story, but she insisted I come over. She assured me she was okay, so I arranged to stop by a couple of hours later. When I pulled up, I saw Grandma

Elena, Clara, and Ralph standing in the street talking. I was sure my presence would not be welcome so I left.

When I called later, she didn't answer. Megan had also called and was unable to reach Grandma Elena. Megan was well aware the city police offered "welfare checks." If a citizen was concerned about not being able to contact a neighbor or friend or family member, the local police encouraged calls, on the police department's business line. The information was given to an officer, and the officer would check to see if there was an emergency situation. Megan decided to ask for a welfare check. The officer made contact with Grandma Elena and Ralph. He called Megan to report that her grandmother would be home soon. He added she should not try to talk to her uncle. According to the officer, Ralph had become unpleasant when the police contacted him.

What was the full story? Grandma Elena and Ralph had gotten into an argument that ended with Grandma Elena threatening to get a gun and shoot Ralph in the head. Then, she threatened to go down to the creek and kill herself. Ralph called the police and asked for a 72-hour hold. The police came to the house and sat with Grandma Elena for about two hours, but found no reason for a mental health evaluation.

To be clear, Grandma Elena did not own a gun, and she was using a walker with limited mobility. She could not have climbed down into the creek, nor did she have access to a car or truck. She was going nowhere. She used the idle threat out of frustration.

When Ralph called Grandma Elena's doctor the next day, he was told the doctor was on vacation. His staff said that if Ralph was concerned about his mother he should take her to the hospital for an evaluation. That is where they were when the officer doing the welfare check contacted Ralph.

I realized Grandma Elena had come close to being removed from her home. So, I sat down to have a heart to heart talk with her. At first, she didn't want to admit to me what the argument was about. I asked what the hospital staff had told her.

"They told me to play nice," she answered.

Exactly what I had been telling her for months, I pointed out. She then got a small grin on her face and said the hospital staff had told Ralph off.

Everyone calmed down and we resumed our routine. I did remind Grandma Elena a few times that she had promised to play nice with Ralph. I also encouraged her to play nice with Rita, reminding her that Rita was just trying to do her job.

Over the next few months, Rita stopped me a couple of times to say, "Grandma Elena really loves you a lot." I appreciated her acknowledgement of the truth and told her that I loved Grandma Elena a lot as well.

In spite of telling the court he had no intention of putting Grandma Elena in a home, in March, Ralph began the process of moving her to a local facility.

One day during lunch, Grandma Elena said, "I'm ready to go. I've finished here and I wouldn't mind going any time."

I asked her about her goal to live to 96 — to be the oldest in her family. She grinned at that reference. I suggested she could make it to 100. Her reply, "That would piss off Ralph."

The last time I visited Grandma Elena at her home was a rainy day. We were sitting in the kitchen chatting when Ralph came in. He stood with his back to the stove and, without a greeting, looked at me.

"Nothing that happens at this house is any of your business." He was almost shouting, he was so angry.

"What?" I had no idea what he was talking about.

"I know you were looking at the construction site next door. You are not to talk to anyone over there or set foot on the site. It is none of your business."

Before coming into Grandma Elena's house, I had stopped to look at the apartment refurbishing project at the end of the street. I hadn't talked to anyone. Even if I had, what business did Ralph have telling me where I could go and who I could talk with?

This outburst brought to mind a saying from Lord Action that Daddy often quoted, "Power tends to corrupt and absolute power corrupts absolutely." I was experiencing the truth of the statement as it unfolded in front of me.

From the look on her face, Grandma Elena was embarrassed by Ralph's behavior. She turned to Ralph and asked, "How did you know she was here?"

Ralph responded, the site manager had called him. He went on to say the site manager called him two or three times a day out of courtesy.

Wow, I thought, Ralph, if you're going to lie make it believable. Why would a construction site manager call someone with no connection to the job? The construction site manager wouldn't have time or a reason to make all those calls and still get his work done.

Then Ralph announced he was leaving, but would stop and see Clara before he returned to work. Yes, we all knew Clara reported all Grandma Elena's activities to Ralph.

The Final Betrayal

*For there to be betrayal,
there would have to have been trust first.*
—Suzanne Collins, *The Hunger Games*

Although we could no longer take Grandma Elena on outings, our visits continued until she fell in January 2015.

I hadn't talked to Grandma Elena for a couple of days because I was preparing for a trip to Africa to teach rural women in Zimbabwe how to can fruit. When I did call, I couldn't get an answer. I called again at dinner time. That time Ralph answered.

"I'm looking for Grandma Elena."

"She's not here."

"When will she be back?"

"Call back in a couple of hours."

"Where is she?"

"I don't know. I have to go." Then he hung up the phone.

How weird. I suspected he knew where she was and just didn't want me to know.

I was having dinner with a friend. I told my friend about the conversation. She said she had seen an ambulance in the neighborhood a couple of days before. I called the local hospital and was told Grandma Elena was no longer there. She had injured her back and had been taken to a convalescent hospital for physical therapy. I found her at the second convalescent hospital I called. The nurse said she would put me through to Grandma Elena's room, but all of a sudden she changed her mind, saying I would have to call back later. I was sure Ralph had blocked my call.

When Megan called asking about Grandma Elena, I told her where she was. Megan then tried to call the convalescent hospital. Ralph blocked the call but not before Grandma Elena heard Megan's name and became upset that she was not allowed to talk to her.

I turned my phone off after dinner, because my friend and I were going to a play. When I turned my phone back on, I found an angry message from Ralph. "You better stop calling. Tell Megan and your friends not to call. You are upsetting her."

I was only able to visit Grandma Elena once before I left for Africa. Grandma Elena explained how she fell on the three steps leading from the kitchen to the garage. She went into the garage to wash her hair every day, do laundry, and get items out of the extra refrigerator. A ramp over those steps would have kept her safe, but Ralph had not provided one. He also had not fixed the flooring in front of the stove where the open seam had become a trip hazard.

Based on my observations, Ralph had not followed any of the recommendations from Pathways to fix trip hazards in his mother's home.

Now, Ralph required he supervise all visits by anyone wanting to see his mother. After my first visit, he refused all my requests, saying he was too busy. During the three weeks I was gone, Megan and Charlotte were each allowed one supervised visit. One of Grandma Elena's friends was also allowed one supervised visit.

During Megan's visit, Ralph provided lunch for Grandma Elena, Megan, and himself on the hospital patio. During lunch, in the presence of his mother, Ralph talked in depth with Megan about renting Grandma Elena's house. He showed her similar houses in the area, pointing out they were renting for $4,000 a month. I'm sure Grandma Elena realized she would not be going home.

When I returned from Africa, Megan let me know that no one knew where Ralph had moved Grandma Elena. Megan had texted Ralph several times, asking about Grandma Elena's location, but he didn't respond. Since I didn't know what else to do, I asked for another "welfare check." I wanted to find out if she was still alive.

The officer went to Grandma Elena's house where he found Ralph, who told the officer that since I had stolen from Grandma Elena, he didn't want to let me see her. Earlier, Ralph had gone to a neighbor and asked if she had been the one to visit Grandma Elena before he moved her. He was upset someone had visited without his supervision. He had accused another neighbor/friend of fronting for me so I could sneak in for an unauthorized visit. Now who was acting paranoid?

While the police kept my name confidential, the contact from the police prompted a nasty call from Ralph's attorney. He demanded to know if I or a member of my family had made the request for a "welfare check."

I told him I wanted to see Grandma Elena and was afraid of losing any chance to see her. The attorney indicated he'd work with the home, Ralph, and the caregivers to set up a visiting schedule, which would be available no later than Monday. By Tuesday, when nothing had arrived I feared they were stalling. I worried she would die before I could see her again. I then called Adult Protective Services to report an elder in isolation.

The schedule arrived at last. I was authorized to see her once a week between 1:00 p.m. and 3:00 p.m., for no more than 30 minutes on Fridays, Saturdays or Sundays.

Adult Protective Services reported to the court because of the conservatorship. The court investigator, Linda Smith, responded she was aware of Grandma Elena's situation and location. She said she would get back to Adult Protective Services with the information so they could close their case. In an email submitted to my attorney by Ralph, Linda Smith asked Ralph where Grandma Elena was located. In spite of my request to remain anonymous, Linda told Ralph that I made the report to Adult Protective Services.

I received another angry phone call from Ralph's attorney. This time, he threatened he would be asking for formal repayment of all gifts Grandma Elena and Papa Frank had made over the last 40 years to me and my family.

By this time, I was beyond frustrated. My primary goal was to visit Grandma Elena. Ralph and his attorney had now gone a step too far. They were now threatening my family. I began in earnest to search for the attorney I'd known years before.

In spite of the care notes on March 5, that didn't mention Ralph's visit, he had Grandma Elena sign a change of beneficiary for her annuity. He removed me, Charlotte, and Megan, and reduced the amount designated for Clara by 5%. He added Rita and took the remainder for himself.

Grandma Elena's signature on the form did not resemble her writing. One of the signatures was not in the proper place on the form.

Ralph arranged for Rita to continue to be responsible for Grandma Elena's care instead of the professional staff at the care home. The care notes written by Rita for March 5 read:

12:00 Mn Changed depend and turn to r. side 2 sips ginger ale, 2 sips of water she's very confuse and asking what's going on

2:30 am refuse to turn

3:30 am turn L. side 1 sip of water She was talking and confuse until sleep

5:00 am Sleep

7:00 am wake up I gave her sponge bath she ate 1 bite of banana.

9:00 am Nurse came give her 2 Tylenol, 1 potassium and 1 Stool softener no problem she did it

9:30 am she thru up & clean her up and report to the nurse.

10:20 am sleep

11:20 am Turn on her back

11:50 am sleep

12:30 pm Nurse came for eye drops and suppository but she refuse.

2:30 pm Refuse to be turn

4:00 pm nurse came she let her do the neb, 1 stool softener, 1 senna pill and the eye drops

5:40 pm Turn on R. side

6:20 pm the nurse put the suppository

7:00 pm turn on her back

8:00 pm she refuse the eye drop

10:00 pm she drink 2 sip of water

11:20 pm turn her on her back.

When I was able to see Grandma Elena in early March, she brightened up when I walked in to her room. We chatted about my trip and I updated her on family activities. Prior to the visit, I had been instructed not to ask any questions. I could not inquire about how she was doing. Nor was I allowed to sit down. Rita was present the whole time butting into our conversation and making sure I didn't ask any questions.

I felt Rita was insensitive to Grandma Elena's need for dignity and privacy. At one point during my visit, Rita interrupted to ask Grandma Elena if she had pooped in her diaper.

I turned to Rita. "You're embarrassing her."

Rita responded, asking Grandma Elena, "Why are you embarrassed? She supposed to be your friend."

I must have different conversations with my friends than Rita had with hers.

I asked Rita if someone could bring Grandma Elena's CD player that Charlotte and Paco had given her, and the CDs from her home.

Since Grandma Elena loved classical music, I thought she would enjoy listening to her favorite CDs. Rita's response was to show me her cell phone. She said she had music on it, and added that Grandma Elena didn't like music.

The flowers I had sent were placed where Grandma Elena could not see them. The only pictures in the room were a double photo frame of Ralph and Gene from their high school years and a snapshot of Grandma Elena's parents. The small picture was so far across the room I had to walk up to it to see the people. When I asked Rita where the picture of Papa Frank was, she snapped, "She don't want that picture." I found that surprising since she had placed it so it was the first thing she saw when she woke up each morning. On my next visit, Papa Frank's picture had appeared.

The next visit to Grandma Elena was disappointing. Rita wouldn't let me wake Grandma Elena. Rita reported she had bathed, shampooed, and changed the bed that morning, leaving Grandma Elena overtired. I found it coincidental since Rita knew I was coming for a visit.

I began to get a lot of criticism from my visits. Ralph's attorney began calling to accuse me of demanding to see Grandma Elena's medical records as well as talking to her doctor. I don't know where he was getting those ideas. Someone was telling lies.

Megan managed to get permission for one visit. It would be her last.

I had had enough of the bullying and I wanted my attorney to step in. He knew me and my family, so when Ralph's attorney started making accusations, my attorney simply asked for the evidence. That stopped Ralph's attorney cold. I regretted not hiring an attorney sooner.

My attorney negotiated one more visit for the Saturday before Easter. I brought a small vase of roses, an Easter card and a book of poems. Even if Grandma Elena was asleep, I had planned to sit by her bed and read some of our favorite poems out loud. I wanted her to feel my love.

But Rita refused to let me see Grandma Elena. I called my attorney and he called Ralph's attorney. This time the return call was from an angry, Ralph. He shouted he would come to the hospital to try to wake his mother and ask her if she wanted a visitor. He would not tell her I was there nor was I to let her know I was there. He continued his tirade. I was not to ask her any financial questions, talk about her estate or about him and his family. At this point, the call dropped. I was devastated. All I wanted was a quiet, loving visit. All the frustration and anger from the past two and half years flooded through me. When I called my attorney, I couldn't explain what had happened. I had no words. I sobbed all the way home.

I did leave the flowers and card for Grandma Elena. Later, Rita sent me a video she had taken with her phone. In it, she kept badgering Grandma Elena to wake up and look at the card and flowers. She ended the video saying to Grandma Elena, "Why would anybody want to visit you when you so sick?" That was the opposite of what I had hoped would happen. Rita later sent me a message saying I could try to visit next week, but I knew that would never happen.

Grandma Elena died on Wednesday, April 8, 2015. There was no memorial or funeral. No celebration of her life of any kind. She was gone.

Grandma Elena had told me she wanted three things at the end of her life:

1. She wanted to live to be 96. That goal was taken away as a result of her fall. It was possible she wouldn't have gotten injured if Ralph had provided a ramp and handrail.

2. She wanted to be surrounded by her friends and loved ones. She specified, she didn't want Ralph, or his family around. Ralph took that away by restricting and denying visits in her last days.

3. She wanted to die in her own bed. Ralph prevented that desire by placing her in a home. The court order said he had to get permission before removing her from her home, but he didn't ask for permission. He just moved her out.

My Anger at the Injustice

Gathering her brows like gathering storm,
Nursing her wrath to keep it warm.
                                    —Robert Burns

After her death, I was angry and tired of being harassed by Ralph and his attorney. I was angry about what Ralph had taken from Grandma Elena and from us. We had lost our time together in her final days and hours. We had lost the opportunity to support her and share our love with her in her final hours.

The primary function of Probate Court is to insure the wishes of the deceased are carried out. Grandma Elena had wanted to disinherit Ralph. He had used the conservatorship to stop her. Now I was willing to fight for what she wanted. I could fight now Grandma Elena was safe and could no longer be hurt.

I gave my attorney all her writings including this note:

June 25, 2012

Preparation notes for very last will

I Elena L Franklin make this my last will and testament and I revoke all former wills and codicils.

I am a widow with two living children
Gene Franklin 9/6/43
Ralph Franklin – 11/26/46

I dispose of all my separate property and entire community and quasi community property to Jo Ann Blum, Charlotte and Megan to share equally.

I give all jewelry, clothing, household furniture and furnishings and personal property not otherwise specifically disposed of to Jo Ann Blum, Charlotte and Megan, also my insurance policies.

I appoint Jo Ann Blum as executor not required to give bond or other securities. If Jo Ann Blum does not want to serve - I appoint Megan to serve as executor.

My executor shall determine any or all expenses of administration of my estate.

Payment of taxes be paid by my executor out of my residue of estate.

I fully and intentionally omitted all persons not mentioned in this will.

Will shall be attested to by Clara - Laura Brown

In witness, thereof I set my hand this 25 day of June 2012

Elena L Franklin

Need attestation of will by two people known to me.

EF

Where should I give instructions for burial? Place etc. How? Who to deliver?

I was ready to fight. I didn't want Ralph to get away with what I felt was bad behavior toward his mother. He had misrepresented and made statements that were untrue about me, my family, and Grandma Elena in order to get his way.

For many technical reasons, however, we didn't prevail in court. Ralph and his family got her estate, but we have our memories as well as the love and support she gave us.

In the 40-plus years I knew Grandma Elena, we never said a cross word to each other. We never raised our voices, and we always had mutual respect and love. I understood how loyal Grandma Elena was.

That loyalty led to the huge argument Grandma Elena had with Sandra and Doris. Grandma Elena expected everyone to be as loyal as she was, and that is part of what blinded her to Ralph's manipulative behavior.

Ralph wasn't always manipulative and angry. When I first met him, before he met his wife, he was a caring, kind, pleasant man. He was careful with his money and loyal to his family. He lived with his parents because, he said then, he liked the companionship. He didn't like living alone in an apartment. Living with his parents meant he was able to save money. He had strong morals and high standards for himself and those around him. Those standards would one day extend to his expectations for his daughters.

The Ralph who returned to California from Tennessee in 2004 was not the same man. Doris told me they had lost a house and a business, loaned money to a friend that caused Ralph and Doris to suffer a huge tax burden. They were forced to file for bankruptcy. One unmarried daughter had a wild episode resulting in a child. Neither daughter finished studies for a college degree. In other words, Ralph had suffered numerous losses and it showed. He appeared to be desperate, bitter, and angry with the world.

The Best of Grandma Elena

The greatest legacy one can pass on to one's children and grandchildren
is not money or other material things accumulated in one's life,
but rather a legacy of character and faith.
—Billy Graham

Ralph may have received Grandma Elena's money and property, but he also had to live with her words.

"Your father would be ashamed of you..."

"... mostly Ralph -- this is the greatest failure of my life

and I failed to recognize warning signs."

My family received the true jewels of Grandma Elena's life. We had her love, emotional support, her encouragement, and the memories we made together over the years.

An example of Grandma Elena's legacy happened when my daughter Charlotte was approached by a co-worker and fellow mom. Alice said she had agreed to make a costume for her son, Drew, to wear in the school play. Alice had attempted to glue the fabric into the shape of a fish, to no avail. Charlotte agreed to sew the costume. When her friend expressed heartfelt gratitude, Charlotte responded, "It's so nice to be able to help someone out using the sewing skills my Grandma taught me."

Not long ago, I was talking to one of my friends when she lamented that since her only child would not have children, she would not have grandchildren. I said to her, "What about the children living next door that you constantly talk about? You get great joy from those children. Why not become their Grandma Elena? It's not possible to have too many grandparents. You can never have too much love in your life."

"The gifts Grandma Elena gave us continue to enrich

our lives daily, proving once again that

love doesn't die, people do."

—R J Blum 2017

The Whole Picture

If there's a single lesson that life teaches us,
it's that wishing doesn't make it so.
—Lev Grossman, *The Magicians*

Numerous circumstances affected what happened to Grandma Elena. When an attorney told me, "Probate Court doesn't like old people," my heart fell. Our experience with the Probate Court supports that opinion. Our probate court did not like old people.

This is what I have learned. A conservatorship is mandated by the probate court to protect adults who are unable to care for themselves. A family member, friend or professional is given the responsibility to provide the needed assistance, and secure the safety of the adult.

Many of us, without investigation, cast votes for a judge. True, judges follow the law, but laws can and are interpreted. In the end, judges depend on the information they are given and rule using their best judgement.

How naïve I was. I now realize not all statements made under oath are true. Some misleading statements made in court are honest errors. Some are out and out lies. In Grandma Elena's case, I believe both were used.

Statements made under the penalty of perjury can be lies. I have been told that perjury is very difficult to prosecute because the attorney must prove intent to deceive and not just a mistake. Those statements are often ignored, making lying under oath less risky.

Another source of frustration is the fact that court appointed attorneys in conservatorship cases may not agree with their clients' wants, and don't fight for their clients' wishes. The idea that everyone is entitled to a defense is a great philosophy, but is not always reality. Once an attorney has been appointed in a conservator case, replacement is not easy.

Ralph went to the probate court to obtain an order for an emergency conservatorship just days after filing for a hearing to become Grandma Elena's conservator. To get the order, he claimed there were irregularities in Grandma Elena's checkbook in spite of also claiming that he had been in charge of her checkbook for the last six years. Grandma Elena was not notified of the request. She was blindsided with no chance to defend herself. In addition, Ralph and his attorney had little evidence to support the allegations they were making. They had Ralph's word, only.

Grandma Elena told me Ralph had demanded to have his name put on her safety deposit box and her household checking account. She also complained he wanted his name on all her accounts, but she felt uncomfortable giving him access to her savings.

That was a two-part move in Grandma Elena's mind.

First, she wanted an excuse to spend time with Ralph in the hope of improving their relationship. As a mother, she wanted to repair the ruptured and fractured relationship that had developed. As an independent woman, she believed she could control the situation.

Second, she thought that by giving in on the safety deposit box and the checking account, Ralph would back off on his demands to have his name on her other accounts. None of this was made clear to the judge. However, the simple act of putting his name on those two accounts made it look as though she had a level of comfort with Ralph accessing her accounts. While the true reasons were never brought out in court, the perception became the important overriding fact.

Here is the first lesson in perception. Grandma Elena should not have allowed herself to be bullied into adding someone's name she didn't trust to her accounts. She should have added someone she trusted to handle her accounts in the event of an emergency, or death. Grandma Elena's later actions indicated she had stopped trusting Ralph. One had to know her and her relationship with Ralph to see the real situation — she hadn't trusted him since he returned from Tennessee.

When the initial report was made to Adult Protective Services, Grandma Elena could have helped her case by being truthful with the examiner.

Grandma Elena had an obligation to herself, and to those who loved her, to be a good consumer of the social support services available. When the information was hidden from the examiner, we couldn't expect them to produce a good and just outcome. Grandma Elena needed to be honest when she accessed the services available to her.

Other things that Grandma Elena could have done to protect herself, included reviewing her entire estate plan to make sure it still represented how she wanted her property distributed. She needed to be sure her choice of the people she wanted in charge of her affairs, should she no longer be capable of handling them herself, was reflected in her estate documents.

After her attorney moved a long distance from her home, making it difficult to visit him, she should have hired another attorney closer to her.

> "The first thing we do,
> let's kill all the lawyers,"
> —Shakespeare's Henry VI

This oft quoted line does a disservice to us all. We need to start looking at lawyers in the same way we look at doctors, as part of our support staff necessary for a full life. Lawyers are not our enemy. Their job is to protect us and advise us on the best way to take care of ourselves and our families.

Grandma Elena should have reviewed the changes in her living situation and asked her attorney for advice on the best way to handle her estate. Attorneys are also referred to as counselors because part of their job is to advise clients of their options as well as the possible consequences.

Grandma Elena often asked for the information she needed in order to give informed consent in medical situations. She understood the importance of being a good consumer of medicine. But she also needed to be an informed consumer of the law.

When Grandma Elena asked if I would be willing to "do this" for her, referring to her Power of Attorney and Durable Power of Attorney for Health Care, I said yes without understanding what it meant. I was not a good consumer of the law. I would never accept a medical procedure without all the information. I now know I needed to apply that standard to the law. We all do.

If Grandma Elena had spent a few hundred dollars asking questions over the years and making sure all her estate papers were in order, she would have saved herself tens of thousands of dollars, and much heartache.

Ralph was able to have her declared incompetent based on his word and the opinion of her doctor because of the papers she had signed. No requirement for testing to see if she was incompetent was outlined in her papers, nor a requirement for an examination by a geriatric specialist. Ralph would never have been able to obtain a conservatorship against her will without the power those papers gave him. She would have remained in control of the end of her life. She would have been able to die in her own home, surrounded by the people who loved her.

If a person has the good fortune to become an elder in our society, that person must face questions about how to live out their final years. If people care about what happens to their estates, it's important to take steps to insure their wishes are followed. Statistics show, most women face those issues alone since their partners often precede them in death.

By sharing our story, I want to start a discussion about expressing our expectations, including how and who we want to assist us in our final years. Parties need to agree and understand how we plan to spend our final years, and when we need them to assist us. As I discovered with Grandma Elena, written documents are not enough. We must have conversations and honest discussions with family in order to avoid misunderstandings. We also need to ensure that the person we have selected to help us agrees with our ideas of how things should be done and will follow through. Since Grandma Elena, did not have these conversations, she lost the right to live her final years the way she wanted.

Sometimes blood relatives don't see eye to eye. The legal definition of family does not mean you like each other or care about each other. Should the quality of relationships be taken into consideration when the question of conservatorship is raised? It is unfair and unhealthy to be forced by a court order to have your life controlled by someone who does not like you. Any person you have told the court you don't want in charge of your affairs and/or your life is not someone who can act as an effective, positive conservator. That's what happened to Grandma Elena.

Sometimes adult children feel they want to take care of parents in their final years. But, when the motive is self-serving, the results can be disastrous for the elder. The time to make sure you remain in charge of your life is not when you are 90, but much, much earlier. Depending on adult children to help can be wonderful — as long as everyone agrees.

When adult children view a parent's estate as their inheritance, they have developed a very dangerous attitude. Ralph said he believed the family trust, set up by Grandma Elena and Papa Frank in 1990, showed how much he and Gene meant to them.

After Grandma Elena fell in January, 2015, at the age of 92, Ralph was able to place her in a care home. Megan told me he claimed the alterations needed to keep her in her own home were too expensive. He wanted to preserve the estate and use the house to generate additional income. In my opinion, he was forgetting the estate was not his, but Grandma Elena's, and should have been used for her care.

I saw Ralph's reluctance to incur the cost of Grandma Elena's care as his interest in not reducing the size of his inheritance. Before assigning a conservator, I wonder if the court should disqualify heirs on the basis of possible conflict of interest.

We are a nation with a growing aging population. When is one an elder? As I write Blessings and Betrayals, the chronological age of 65 years is the most common indicator of an older status in the United States. Seniors make up 13.3% of the population. Florida has the highest percent of seniors with 18%. Pennsylvania and West Virginia each have 15% of their population made up of seniors. The largest number of seniors resides in California. Many families, individuals, and couples will face the same issues that Grandma Elena and my family faced. Of those who face these issues, the largest portion will be widows. Women in the United States are expected, on an average, to live 81.3 years while men live 76.3 years.

As you read this story, I hope it became clear how important it is to review estate plans in order to avoid problems and remain in control of your destiny. While we review our plan for our final years, and who we will trust to take care of us and our estate, we must look at those around us with clear eyes. No matter how painful it is to admit, some relationships are not as healthy as we believe they should be, so we must protect ourselves.

Our courts assume our closest blood relatives are the natural objects of our affection. I find it sad, when that is not always the case. If we want someone other than relatives, we must set things up with care and review them often so the court has a clear picture of our intent.

The fault did not fall only on Grandma Elena. The system failed her. Her court appointed attorney believed the story Ralph and his attorney told him. Had he asked for back up to their allegations as my attorney later did, he would have seen the case in a new light. If you believe our system is set up so even murderers get a vigorous defense, then Grandma Elena got shortchanged. If Ralph had been unable to obtain an emergency conservatorship or if the emergency conservatorship had still allowed Grandma Elena to retain counsel of choice, the story would have had a different ending.

The bottom line is we should be asking our legislators to review this system to ensure it doesn't happen to others. No one should be prevented from retaining the attorney of their choice.

Recognizing that older people thrive better when they are allowed full access to visits and phone calls, California passed a law to prevent conservators or anyone else from isolating seniors. However, the law is ineffective if it is not enforced. One police officer I spoke to indicated isolation was not considered when investigating suspected abuse.

When Ralph's visit restrictions were brought to the court investigator's attention, she told Ralph on several occasions that he needed to lift the restrictions. Grandma Elena's attorney also wrote to Ralph's attorney demanding the restrictions be removed.

No one followed up to determine if the restrictions had been removed. As a result, Ralph was able to control access to Grandma Elena. Once she was in the care home her phone calls were also cut off.

Grandma Elena did not receive the booklet explaining her rights under a conservatorship. That was the responsibility of her attorney. I believe, had she understood what a conservatorship was, Ralph could not have kept her from exercising her rights under the law. Included in the rights she retained was the right to vote and to make changes to her estate. She also had the right to leave her house anytime with anyone. I believe Ralph was aware Grandma Elena had retained those rights and that knowledge was why he was so upset each time someone visited whom he didn't know.

Judges depend on court investigators to provide fair and impartial reports. In cases involving seniors, establishing trust is important. When the investigator shows up, along with the opposing party and a uniformed police officer, the trust is lost. Grandma Elena saw the court investigator's visit as part of the opposition. When asked questions, I believe Grandma Elena was afraid to give honest answers, claiming instead that she did not remember. She was aware Ralph had brought the case for conservatorship to stop her from making the changes to her estate plan.

It should also be policy for the investigator to interview seniors when they are well rested not tired or under duress, which may require more time to investigate. Remember, the investigation conducted by the court will impact the life of individuals and their families. When hearing conflicting stories, more time to investigate may be needed. In Grandma Elena's case, friends and neighbors could have provided a fuller picture. Once the investigator gave Ralph her personal cell phone number, all appearance of being impartial was lost.

Nor can Adult Protective Services serve the community by deferring to the court when the report of suspected abuse involves a conservator. If a full investigation had been conducted, the isolation Grandma Elena experienced would have been uncovered. By law, institutions are not allowed to restrict visits without a court order. By allowing Ralph to demand he supervise all visits and cut off her free access to phone calls, Grandma Elena was imprisoned.

When you build a loving relationship, both sides gain. When a relationship deteriorates, both parties lose. That's what happened to Ralph, his family, and Grandma Elena. The loss creates its own pain. Grandma Elena recognized this when she said, "Ralph and Doris kept their girls away from me and they lost what I had to give." Grandma Elena also lost the joy of a close relationship with them.

What happened over the last 40 plus years may be unique in detail, but the fact remains relationships evolve and change. People drift apart whether they are related by blood or not. Others foster a closer and closer bond. The way you envision the end of your life, including the people supporting you, can evolve over time. Relationships and economic realities in your 60's can be different from those you face in your 90's.

A word of warning. Individuals wishing to control your life and estate won't show their intentions until you are vulnerable. Under the law, knowledge is power. We need to ask questions, understand the power of the papers we sign, review plans often, and demand the best from our courts and safety agencies. For the benefit of your loved ones and your ability to be with them in a healthy and supportive manner, learn from this story, and avoid getting caught in the same trap that ensnared Grandma Elena.

Goodbye, Grandma Elena

Goodbye, Grandma Elena.
You'll live on in our hearts
And the brightest stars will spell out your name
And the joy you brought us will be remembered every day.

The letters you wrote
Made me smile every time
And all the puzzles you gave us
Were fun and challenging.

Oh, the times we spent
Singing in the yard
And the gopher holes and birds
We watched together.

The lemons we picked like flowers
Fell heavy in the paper bag
And the oranges we picked
Were the sweetest I ever had.

Goodbye, Grandma.
You'll live on in our hearts
And the joy you brought us
Will be remembered every day
Oh, thank you, stars, for spelling out her name.

Ana, age 11

Letter to Grandma Elena

Dear Grandma Elena:

I miss you every day. There is always something happening that I want to share with you. I want to sit at your kitchen table again — talk and laugh. I carry you in my heart. You are there with all the beautiful memories we made together. I am grateful I was able to thank you for teaching me how to be a grandmother as I said goodbye to you the last time. I am confident you know we wanted to be with you in your last days and hours.

I will always regret I was not able to protect you. I am sorry that I didn't listen, when you complained about Ralph, and how he treated you until it was too late. Everything you predicted Ralph would do, he did. Now I will tell our story to help others avoid our mistakes.

You taught me so many things. My family and I are the greater for having known you. Words cannot describe how your friendship and love have blessed our lives. How much it meant to have you as grandmother to my children, and great-grandmother to my grandchildren, and an amazing special friend to me.

You lived a good and interesting life.

Rest in peace without worries or cares.

With eternal love and admiration,

Jo Ann

Resources and Suggestions

Everyone has a responsibility to report any suspicion of elder abuse, protecting one protects all. Responsible reporting includes all evidence of abuse. Bullies feed on the weakness of others. Everyone ages differently. Some of us will grow gradually weaker as we age and some will weaken more quickly. It is as we weaken that we become vulnerable.

The following are some national and state organizations working to help prevent elder abuse.

1. National Adult Protective Services Association
   www.napsa-now.org

2. National Consumer Voice for Quality Long Term Care
   www.caregiver.org

3. CA Advocates for Nursing Home Reform
   www.canhr.org

4. Local Law Enforcement (will provide "welfare checks")

Become an informed consumer of our laws. Ask questions when asked to sign documents so all the powers included in the documents are clear. Also have an understanding of what is expected, before accepting responsibilities to help.

When I was in college a friend's father, who knew he was dying, went to his attorney and made sure his entire estate was organized the way he wanted. The father then wrote a letter to his wife and adult children outlining his final wishes, which he placed in his safety deposit box. This letter included where all his assets were, how to contact his attorney, and his personal wishes for his funeral, which included the mortuary to use, music, and people to speak, all the details. He outlined exactly how he wanted his personal property distributed. The letter was dated and signed, he reviewed it every six months and wrote a few updated lines indicating anything he had forgotten and confirming the plans. He included a personal note for each family member.

At the writing of Blessings and Betrayals a self-video would be an easy effective way to communicate final wishes and loving messages. Ask an estate attorney for guidelines.

An estate planning attorney can be found by checking the American Bar Association web-site

www.americanbar.org/directories/lawyer-referral-directory.html

Or ask family and friends for referrals.

CPSIA information can be obtained
at www.ICGtesting.com
Printed in the USA
FSHW02n0617090518
47979FS